D0400747

SUPREME COURT DECISIONS

EDITED WITH AN INTRODUCTION BY
JAY M. FEINMAN

SERIES EDITOR
RICHARD BEEMAN

PENGUIN BOOKS

PENGUIN BOOKS
Published by the Penguin Group
Penguin Group (USA) Inc., 375 Hudson Street, New York, New York 10014, U.S.A.
Penguin Group (Canada), 90 Eglinton Avenue East, Suite 700, Toronto, Ontario,
Canada M4P 2Y3 (a division of Pearson Penguin Canada Inc.)
Penguin Books Ltd, 80 Strand, London WC2R 0RL, England
Penguin Ireland, 25 St Stephen's Green, Dublin 2, Ireland
(a division of Penguin Books Ltd)
Penguin Group (Australia), 250 Camberwell Road, Camberwell, Victoria 3124,
Australia (a division of Pearson Australia Group Pty Ltd)
Penguin Books India Pvt Ltd, 11 Community Centre,
Panchsheel Park, New Delhi - 110 017, India
Penguin Group (NZ), 67 Apollo Drive, Rosedale, Auckland 0632, New Zealand
(a division of Pearson New Zealand Ltd)
Penguin Books (South Africa) (Pty) Ltd, 24 Sturdee Avenue, Rosebank,
Johannesburg 2196, South Africa

Penguin Books Ltd, Registered Offices:
80 Strand, London WC2R 0RL, England

First published in Penguin Books 2012

13   15   17   19   20   18   16   14   12

Book introduction, notes, and abridgment copyright © Jay M. Feinman, 2012
Series introduction copyright © Richard Beeman, 2012
All rights reserved

No copyright is claimed on works of the United States Government.

LIBRARY OF CONGRESS CATALOGING-IN-PUBLICATION DATA

Supreme Court decisions / edited with an introduction by Jay M. Feinman.
p.   cm.—(Penguin civic classics)
ISBN 978-0-14-312199-2
1. Constitutional law—United States—Cases.   I. Feinman, Jay M.
II. United States. Supreme Court.
KF4550.S835 2012
342.73—dc23   2012023218

Printed in the United States of America
Set in Adobe Caslon
Designed by Sabrina Bowers

ALWAYS LEARNING   PEARSON

CONTENTS

SERIES
INTRODUCTION

W e introduce the Penguin Civic Classics series by presenting our readers with a paradox. On the one hand, there is an
abundance of evidence establishing that the vast majority of Americans, whatever their political differences, have an intense love of their country, believing
that it has been one of the most successful experiments
in human freedom and opportunity that the world has
ever seen. And Americans are similarly united in having a deep reverence for their Constitution, for their
institutions of government, and for the system of free
enterprise that has been such a powerful engine for our
economic growth. Americans see all of these as playing
a vital role in making the nation as successful as it has
been.

But there is an equally large body of evidence sug-
gesting that Americans' knowledge of their history and
of the way in which their institutions have worked over
the course of that history is embarrassingly meager. For
example, a third of Americans believe that the Declaration of Independence was written after the end of the
Civil War, and fewer than half can identify the three

branches of our federal government. Nearly 40 percent of the students at fifty-five of America's elite colleges and universities could not place the Civil War in the correct half century, and fewer than half of them, when presented with the text of the Gettysburg Address, were able to identify it. Nor does it appear that our knowledge improves much as we move closer to the present. Another survey has revealed that more than half of high school seniors thought that Italy, Germany, or Japan was a U.S. ally during the Second World War, and only 14 percent of those seniors could name any relevant fact about U.S. involvement in the Korean War. As the distinguished historian David Mc-Cullough has lamented, "While the clamorous popular culture races on, the American past is slipping away, out of sight and out of mind. We are losing our story, forgetting who we are and what it's taken to come this far."

With these discouraging results in front of us, it is no wonder that there is a growing clamor for an increased emphasis on "civic education," defined by one leading authority as "the cultivation of the virtues, knowledge, and skills" necessary for carrying out one's role as a citizen. That very phrase, "civic education," sounds to many like a doctor's prescription: "You need to take your medicine! It may not be very pleasant, but it is something you need to do in order to ensure not only your own health but also the health of the body politic." It is our hope that reading these volumes in the Penguin Civic Classics series will be much more pleasant than taking medicine, for although these volumes will indeed help improve the reader's civic *knowledge*, we also hope that they will provide some civic *inspira-*

tion—a genuine appreciation for, even an excitement about, some of the words, ideas, and actions that have shaped American society and government since the nation's founding.

The history represented in these volumes, from the founding of the American colonies in the seventeenth century to the adoption of America's Declaration of Independence to Abraham Lincoln's inspiring Gettysburg Address to Barack Obama's inaugural address as the first African American president in American history, is not merely a collection of names and dates to be memorized but, rather, a set of stories to be absorbed and enjoyed. And they are stories that have a real relevance and meaning to our lives today, whether we are debating the nature of America's immigration laws, the extent to which the federal government should be involved in decisions relating to our health care, or, getting even closer to home, whether local schools and school districts have the constitutional right to search a student's locker.

In these volumes, the reader will encounter nearly all the central themes in American history, as well as the dilemmas and conflicts that have provided much of the dynamism and excitement of that history. The central themes and ideas of American public life—democracy, equality, economic opportunity, the role of government in maintaining that delicate balance between public order and personal freedom, and the government's responsibility to protect certain individual rights—have never remained static, nor have they ever elicited uniform agreement among American citizens.

The very first item in Terry Golway's collection of important American speeches is a sermon given by

Massachusetts governor John Winthrop, aboard the ship *Arbella*, as it transported the first Puritan settlers to the new colony. In that sermon, Winthrop described the Puritans' mission in Massachusetts Bay as one of creating a "city upon a hill," a model of virtue and purity for all others in the world to follow. But his vision of that society was in some important respects very much at odds with the values that guide America today. In the opening words of his sermon, Winthrop reminded his fellow colonists that "GOD ALMIGHTY in His most holy and wise providence, hath so disposed of the condition of mankind, as in all times some must be rich, some poor, some high and eminent in power and dignity; others mean and in submission." Hardly a prescription for the democratic society that we claim to be today.

Fast-forward 136 years to the promise contained in Thomas Jefferson's Declaration of Independence that "all men are created equal"—a view of society *very* different from that articulated by Winthrop. Jefferson's city upon a hill was to be a nation dedicated to equality and the pursuit of happiness, not to a divinely ordained, inegalitarian social hierarchy. But, of course, in a world in which Africans were enslaved, women were considered legally subordinate to men, and, indeed, many free white males were denied the right to vote because they did not own the requisite amount of property, Jefferson's promise of equality fell far short of an accurate description of the reality of American society in 1776. Still, words have power, and Abraham Lincoln, for one, knew the power of those words. As is amply displayed in Allen Guelzo's volume containing many of Lincoln's principal speeches, time and time again Lincoln invoked Jefferson's preamble as a pledge that Americans of his age were honor-bound to fulfill, describing the preamble as "the electric cord in that Declaration that links the hearts of patriotic and liberty-loving men together, that will link those patriotic hearts as long as the love of freedom exists in the minds of men throughout the world."

Alas, Americans would fight a horrific, bloody civil war in which more than 600,000 people, slave and free, lost their lives before the nation was able to take the steps necessary to forge the link to which Lincoln had referred. Beginning in December 1865, with the adoption of the Thirteenth Amendment, eliminating the institution of slavery; continuing with the adoption of the Fourteenth Amendment (July 1868), with its guarantee of "equal protection under the laws"; and culminating with the adoption of the Fifteenth Amendment (February 1870), asserting that the right to vote could not "be abridged ... on account of race, color, or previous condition of servitude," those ideas of democracy and equality began to be incorporated into our constitutional system. But although those three amendments represented an important step forward, America's struggle to live up to the promise of the preamble was far from over. It took until 1920 for the nation to adopt the Nineteenth Amendment, giving women the right to vote, and in spite of the guarantees of the Fourteenth and Fifteenth Amendments, the civil rights of African Americans, including the right to vote, continued to be undermined by the actions of individual state governments well into the twentieth century. When Lyndon Johnson, only the second (after Woodrow Wilson) Southern-born president since the

Civil War, signed into law the Voting Rights Act of 1965, he too quoted the preamble to the Declaration of Independence and ended his speech with a phrase from the anthem of the civil rights movement of the 1950s and 1960s: "We Shall Overcome." And when the first African American president, Barack Obama, delivered his inauguration speech on a cold day in January 2009, he began by paraphrasing the words of Thomas Jefferson's preamble, urging Americans "to carry forward that precious gift, that noble idea, passed on from generation to generation: the God-given promise that all are equal, all are free, and all deserve a chance to pursue their full measure of happiness." Even in 2009 those words were, like Jefferson's, expressions of hope, not descriptions of reality. But they have proved powerful indeed, and they continue to be a dynamic force in shaping the American future just as they have the American past.

Another important theme that emerges from these volumes of Civic Classics involves the age-old debate on how and where to strike the best balance between public order and personal liberty. For most of human history, those who held government power—kings or emperors or czars—usually dealt with that issue by ruthlessly imposing their own definition of what was good for the masses of people whom they governed. When Thomas Paine published his earth-shaking pamphlet *Common Sense* in January 1776, his primary purpose was to persuade the American colonists to throw off British rule, but one of the key elements in his argument was the notion that while every society needs some form of government in order to provide security and protect the freedom of its citizens, the best and freest societies are those in which government is least intrusive. In Paine's words: "Society in every state is a blessing, but government even in its best state is but a necessary evil; in its worst state an intolerable one." Paine's words struck a chord with his American readers, who were already suspicious of the overly powerful, distant government of Great Britain, and the Declaration of Independence, approved seven months later, reinforced that same theme. The distrust of concentrations of government power—the notion that government, while necessary, must be restrained—is deeply rooted in America's revolutionary past and, of course, is very much alive today, as we can observe by the vitality of political movements such as the Tea Party.

As powerful as Paine's and Jefferson's indictments of excessive British power may have been, they did not provide the answer to the question of how the independent American nation could create a government that would strike an ideal balance between order and liberty. The men who gathered in Philadelphia in the summer of 1787 to frame a new constitution for their still-fragile independent nation took a giant step forward in providing an answer when they created a governmental system based on the division of power between the individual states and the central government—the system that we now call federalism—and by further dividing power among the three branches of the federal government in a system that we characterize as one of "checks and balances."

But, as in so many other important ideas in American history, those involving federalism and checks and balances were subject to many different interpretations. Alexander Hamilton, James Madison, and John Jay, in the eighty-five essays comprising *The Federalist Papers,* attempted to address some of the concerns that Americans had about the excessive power of the proposed new federal government and, in the process, provided Americans with enduring insights about government and politics—insights that are still cited by Supreme Court justices in their judicial opinions today. But Hamilton and Madison, the two principal authors of *The Federalist Papers,* began to disagree about the relationship of the new federal government to the individual states and to the people at large almost from the moment the government commenced operation. The debate over the way the words of the Constitution should be interpreted, with Madison and Jefferson taking a "strict construction" position, and Hamilton, George Washington, and others arguing for a broader interpretation of the Constitution, has stayed with us until the present day. As readers of Jay Feinman's collection of landmark Supreme Court cases will discover, the Court has spent a significant portion of its time over the years, beginning with Chief Justice John Marshall's majority opinion in *McCulloch v. Maryland* (1819), wrestling with the extent of and limits on federal government power. Nor has that conflict been confined to judicial or intellectual arguments. In the years leading up to the Civil War, Northern and Southern politicians fought ferocious battles over the question of what authority the federal government had to legislate with respect to the expansion of slavery into new territories; once again, the ever-eloquent Abraham Lincoln weighed in on those issues, as is amply illustrated in Allen Guelzo's selection of Lincoln speeches. In the end, of course, it was not words that settled the constitutional argument between North and South but the force of arms. The Civil War was, in some senses, America's greatest civic failure, for knowledge and reason alone were not sufficient to settle the conflict between North and South. But however terrible the toll, it did resolve the paradox at the nation's core—the existence of the institution of slavery in a nation that claimed to be devoted to liberty.

Mercifully, the Civil War was the last occasion in which our differences of opinion over governmental power have resulted in warfare, but the war of words has never ceased. Whether debating issues relating to economic regulation or immigration, or providing and regulating health care, Americans—Republicans and Democrats, Tea Party members and Occupy Wall Street activists—continue to differ, sometimes passionately, on the way our Constitution should be interpreted.

Americans, perhaps more than any other people in the world, have been ardently committed to defending their "rights." Indeed, when most Americans today think of their Constitution, they think not so much about those enumerated powers such as the levying of taxes, the regulating of commerce, or the coining of money that are contained in the main body of the Constitution, but, rather, they think of the Bill of Rights. In fact, one of the few mistakes made by the framers of the Constitution in 1787 was their failure even to include a Bill of Rights in their final draft of the Constitution, a mistake that was, fortunately, remedied by the First Federal Congress in 1789. The rights articulated in our first ten amendments, including freedom of speech, the "free exercise of religion," freedom of the press, and freedom from unlawful search and seizure, have not only provided the foundation for the freedoms that we so value today but have also prompted some of our most vigorously debated controversies. Readers of Jay Feinman's volume on some of the most important Supreme Court decisions in our history will discover that, in general, the Court's definition of the rights guaranteed in those amendments has tended to widen over the course of our history. But there remain limits on the Bill of Rights protections enjoyed by Americans. For example, the right of free speech has not extended to public protests in which the threat of violence is imminent, and in an era of GPS tracking devices and CCTV cameras, Americans are confronted with new challenges in defining what constitutes an unlawful search and seizure.

The constitutional protection of individual rights has not been confined to those items specifically listed in the Bill of Rights. The Ninth Amendment, which says that the "enumeration in the Constitution, of certain rights, shall not be construed to deny or disparage others retained by the people," has been interpreted to include the right of privacy, including the right of a woman to have some control over her health and reproductive decisions. The most well known of the Supreme Court decisions relating to the right of a woman to terminate a pregnancy, *Roe v. Wade* (1973), far from settling that difficult question, has been followed by a series of subsequent Supreme Court decisions seeking to further refine and, in many cases, limit the right to obtain an abortion. The Court's decisions in these areas, far from being legal abstractions of interest only to a few history or civics teachers, have had an impact, and will continue to have an impact, on the lives of millions of women.

This series of Penguin Civic Classics is based on the belief that acquiring knowledge of America's history and of our rights and responsibilities as citizens is not merely an abstract, academic exercise. *It really matters.* It can make an actual difference in each and every one of our lives. And never more so than in the extraordinarily complicated, tumultuous, twenty-first-century world in which we live—a time of rapid, sometimes confounding, change. David McCullough has spoken of the way in which our knowledge of history and of the way in which our institutions of government operate can give us a "sense of navigation, a sense of what we've been through in times past and who we are." It can also *empower* us. If we are familiar with the way in which people in the past have confronted their problems, and if we have a decent understanding of how to make the best use of America's institutions to deal with the problems confronting us in the present, we have a much better chance of being able to control our own destinies. Our opinions of the "correct" way to proceed may not always prevail, but we will at least be participants, not passive bystanders, in the ongoing drama that is the history of the United States. And, perhaps most important of all, it is often personally more rewarding, more fun, to be a participant rather than to be a bystander.

RICHARD BEEMAN

INTRODUCTION

The Supreme Court of the United States is a remarkable institution. In a democratic nation in which elections are hotly contested and scores of politicians are swept into office and then out again, the Supreme Court is composed of nine justices who are appointed for life and usually serve for decades. Although the judicial branch has been called "the least dangerous branch" of government, the decisions of the Court on issues of constitutional law are binding, invalidating statutes passed by Congress or state legislatures and even limiting the president's powers as commander in chief. And despite the twenty-four-hour news cycle in which politicians become celebrities and political events are featured on television and the Internet, the Court's sessions are not televised and its justices are seldom seen or heard in public.

The Court's most important job is to interpret and apply the provisions of the United States Constitution. In doing so, it has to do what all courts do: state what the law is and apply its statement of the law to resolve a dispute. But that is not all that it does. In expressing its view of constitutional law, the Court also makes important statements about American civic values. The Court's decisions speak to what our most fundamental beliefs are, what we want government to do and not do, even who we are as a people.

The Court can speak so broadly because the Constitution has such a wide reach. Drafted in 1787, the Constitution contains fewer than 4,400 words, about the length of fifteen pages in this book. The Bill of Rights (the first ten amendments to the Constitution) was added in 1791, and only seventeen more amendments have been added in the more than two centuries since. Yet the Constitution is, as it proclaims itself, "the supreme law of the land." Everything that is done by every level of government must be consistent with the Constitution. Can a town put a Christmas display in a public park? Can the federal government require individuals to purchase health insurance? Can the military detain an American citizen as an enemy combatant? The Constitution, as interpreted by the Supreme Court, gives the final answer. And most significant political issues eventually come to the Court as questions of constitutional law. Before the Civil War it was the constitutionality of slavery and of Congress's attempts to find compromise between North and South; today it is the constitutionality of the regulation of abortion and of campaign finance.

The Court does not have an easy task in deciding questions such as these. What makes it particularly difficult is that all the answers have to start by reference to a particular, narrow source—the text of the Constitution and its amendments. Sometimes everyone understands the text the same way. Article II requires that no one may be president who has not "attained to the age of thirty-five years," so it would be hard to argue that even an exceptionally mature thirty-year-old could be elected to the presidency. Sometimes everyone understands that the text does not mean what it appears to mean on its face. The First Amendment begins, "*Congress* shall make no law respecting an establishment of religion, or prohibiting the free exercise thereof," but even the strictest of strict constructionists acknowledges that the amendment also prevents the president from infringing a person's religious freedom. But these are the cases that are so easy that they never come to the Court. Much more often the constitutional text demands extensive interpretation because it is vague and its application to a particular set of facts is uncertain. Does the First Amendment's prohibition of an establishment of religion prevent a middle school from having a rabbi deliver a nonsectarian invocation at its graduation ceremony?

In attempting to give content to the text, the justices take different approaches. Some try to divine the original understanding of the framers of the Constitution or of the legislatures that ratified it. Others look to principles embodied in the text or the way its meaning has been understood in light of changes in society over time. Whatever their approaches, however, the justices use the constitutional text and the sources of interpretation to express civic values. The Constitution can be understood only in context, and that context—or those contexts, in the case of disagreement—entails a vision of the American political and social community.

Consider as an example the first case excerpted in chapter 1, *McCulloch v. Maryland*. In the early decades of the Republic, the nature of the new national government was an issue of great public moment. In an opinion by Chief Justice John Marshall, the Court held that the national government is a government of limited powers, authorized to do only what the Constitution empowers it to do. However, the government is not restricted to a narrow view of those powers; instead, the Constitution authorizes it to do whatever is "necessary and proper" to carry out its responsibilities, and "necessary" implies using "any means calculated to produce the end" and does not mean "absolutely necessary." When the national government exercises its constitutional authority, the states may not interfere because the Constitution grants the national government supremacy within its sphere of authority. This was the Court's statement of constitutional principle, and it had a particular consequence in the case: The State of Maryland could not impose a tax on the Second Bank of the United States, which was chartered by Congress.

McCulloch v. Maryland is more than a conclusion about the power of Maryland to tax a federal entity; it is an expression of our view about government. Government is instituted by the people to achieve the common good, and it is both empowered to achieve that good and restricted to prevent it from doing harm. The federal government, for example, is a government of enumerated powers and so is limited to issues with which the people have entrusted it. But government needs to be effective, so within the scope of its authority the government is not limited to acts absolutely necessary for the fulfillment of its role; instead, it can do what needs to be done to achieve the common good. The powers conferred on Congress by the Constitution to "regulate commerce" and to "borrow money" are reasonably exercised by the chartering of a national bank and are therefore "necessary and proper" for government to do its work.

McCulloch v. Maryland did not settle the issue of the scope of government power for all time, of course. Even today, libertarians take a limited view of government's role and progressives an expansive one, and the scope of the Commerce Clause continues to be litigated in the Supreme Court. These controversies show that the Court's explication of civic values is never complete, definitive, or final. Instead, the Court's opinions are part of an ongoing conversation about politics and society.

The fact that the conversation is always in flux is most evident in the civil rights cases excerpted in chapter 4. In *Scott v. Sandford* (the *Dred Scott* case) in 1857, the Court held that blacks were a "subordinate and inferior class of beings" who could never be members of the American political community and had only such rights as "those who held the power" might choose to give them. The Civil War and the Reconstruction Amendments changed that status, but often in form more than in substance. In *Plessy v. Ferguson* in 1896, the Court upheld a Louisiana law requiring separate but equal seating for black and white railroad passengers. "If the civil and political rights of both races be equal," Justice Henry Billings Brown wrote, "one cannot be inferior to the other civilly or politically." Six decades later, of course, "separate but equal" fell through the Court's decision in *Brown v. Board of Education*. Segregation of black children, even in nominally equal schools, "generates a feeling of inferiority as to their status in the community that may affect their hearts and minds in a way unlikely ever to be undone," wrote Chief Justice Earl Warren for a unanimous Court.

Plessy v. Ferguson also illustrates that the conversation about civic values can be contested at any one moment as well as changing over time. In that case Justice John Marshall Harlan famously dissented from the Court's opinion, arguing that American values after the Civil War called for a color-blind society. The Constitution, he wrote, does not "permit any public authority to know the race" of an individual in the protection of rights. Formal equality was not enough, particularly where "everyone knows" that the Louisiana statute was enacted to favor whites at the expense of blacks. And, appealing to a history that would come to pass in *Brown*, he predicted that "the judgment this day rendered will, in time, prove to be quite as pernicious as the decision made by this tribunal in the *Dred Scott Case.*"

Dissents and historical changes demonstrate that the Supreme Court's statements of values are rich and diverse. Each of the chapters in this book provides excerpts of the Court's opinions on different topics. They do not offer a comprehensive introduction to constitutional law, and on all the topics there are many more cases and more recent cases. Instead, they give an introduction to the justices' thinking on some of our most fundamental civic principles. Sometimes the justices proclaim values most strongly when they disagree among themselves, and for that reason the book includes famous dissents. In chapter 2, for example, the opinion of the Court in *Abrams v. United States* is no longer the law and is remembered only by constitutional scholars. Justice Holmes's dissent in that case, however, created the concept of free speech as a "marketplace of ideas," a concept that still has vitality.

Chapter 1 discusses the nature of American government. To accomplish things together that we could not do individually—build roads and schools, ensure the safety of prescription drugs, protect against criminals, terrorists, and hostile nations, and do so much more—we establish and support government. To accomplish all these ends, government must be strong. But a government that is strong enough to do what it needs to do is also a threat to do things that we don't want and to infringe on our rights. The cases excerpted in chapter 1 are among the Supreme Court's attempts to define the proper scope of government. Among the famous principles expressed in these cases is that ours is "a government of laws, and not of men" (*Marbury v. Madison*), that we are a single union, not simply a collection of states, in which the federal government is a "government of all; its powers are delegated by all; it represents all, and acts for all" (*McCulloch v. Maryland*), and that "a state of war is not a blank check for the President when it comes to the rights of the Nation's citizens" (*Hamdi v. Rumsfeld*).

Chapter 2 addresses the freedom of speech guaranteed by the First Amendment. The chapter begins with a case in which the majority of the Court limited free speech but Justice Holmes famously dissented, arguing that the "best test of truth" lies in the marketplace of ideas, in which different beliefs compete for public favor (*Abrams v. United States*). This competition is essential to our political process, for we have "a profound national commitment to the principle that debate on public issues should be uninhibited, robust, and wide-open" (*New York Times v. Sullivan*) because "the right of citizens to inquire, to hear, to speak, and to use information to reach consensus is a precondition to enlightened self-government and a necessary means to protect it" (*Citizens United v. Federal Election Commission*). Free speech is also important so that people can fulfill their own life goals; the framers of the Constitution "believed liberty to be the secret of happiness" (*Whitney v. California*).

Freedom of religion is the subject of chapter 3. The First Amendment expresses two principles about religion and the state: The government may neither "establish" a religion nor prohibit the "free exercise" of religion. Each is equally important. The Establishment Clause creates "a wall of separation between Church and State" (*Everson v. Board of Education*) because "a union of government and religion tends to destroy government and to degrade religion" (*Engel v. Vitale*). The Free Exercise Clause creates space for individuals to practice their own faith: "The government may not compel affirmation of religious belief, punish the expression of religious doctrines it believes to be false, impose special disabilities on the basis of religious views or religious status, or lend its power to one or the other side in controversies over religious authority or dogma" (*Employment Division v. Smith*).

All the issues discussed in the book are contentious, but chapter 4 covers the area that has been most contentious and most subject to change: civil rights. Prior to the Civil War, the Court held that even free blacks were not "part of the people" who had rights under the Constitution (*Scott v. Sandford*), a position that was not fully changed until the Court declared in *Brown v. Board of Education* that "the doctrine of 'separate but equal'" had no place in public education. *Brown* did not settle all questions of race relations, of course. "The Constitution abhors classifications based on race," wrote Justice Thomas in dissent in *Grutter v. Bollinger*, but the majority in that case held that racial classifications are constitutional "if they are narrowly tailored to further compelling governmental interests."

Chapter 5 discusses the right of privacy, the most expansive right protected by the Constitution and one that draws on many other rights for inspiration and definition. "It is a promise of the Constitution that there is a realm of personal liberty which the government may not enter," and the right of privacy fulfills that promise (*Planned Parenthood v. Casey*). This right includes "the right of the individual to contract, to engage in any of the common occupations of life, to acquire useful knowledge, to marry, establish a home and bring up children, to worship God according to the dictates of his own conscience, and generally to enjoy those privileges long recognized at common law as essential to the orderly pursuit of happiness by free men" (*Meyer v. Nebraska*).

Chapter 6 concludes the book by examining basic values that are incorporated in the criminal and civil justice systems. These are the arenas in which the government can deprive people of their liberty or provide a forum for the allocation of legal rights, and our values require that those arenas be fair and open, and that requirement is based on the concept of personal rights. Accordingly, "[t]he efforts of the courts and their officials to bring the guilty to punishment, praiseworthy as they are, are not to be aided by the sacrifice of those great principles established by years of endeavor and suffering which have resulted in their embodiment in the fundamental law of the land" (*Weeks v. United States*). Sometimes this means that "[t]he criminal goes free, if he must, but it is the law that sets him free. Nothing can destroy a government more quickly than its failure to observe its own laws" (*Mapp v. Ohio*). In the civil justice system, "persons forced to settle their claims of right and duty through the judicial process must be given a meaningful opportunity to be heard" (*Boddie v. Connecticut*).

JAY M. FEINMAN

A NOTE ON THE TEXT

The Supreme Court opinions in this book have been heavily edited for ease of reading and to focus on the Court's expression of values rather than on its detailed analysis of the facts and law. Omissions are not indicated by ellipses. Each opinion is preceded by a short editorial note explaining its facts and context.

Chapter 1
GOVERNMENT

McCULLOCH V. MARYLAND,
17 U.S. 316 (1819)

☞ The Constitution was framed and ratified to cure the problems created by the lack of a strong central government and the disunion under the Articles of Confederation. But ratification did not end the controversies over government powers. *McCulloch v. Maryland* was one of a series of decisions by the Supreme Court in the early years of the Republic that addressed those controversies.

Congress chartered the Second Bank of the United States in 1816, and the bank established branches in many cities, including Baltimore. The Maryland legislature adopted a tax on the bank, enforceable by a penalty on the officers of the bank. The state brought an action to enforce the penalty after James McCulloch, the cashier of the Baltimore branch of the Bank of the United States, refused to comply with the Maryland law. In an opinion by Chief Justice John Marshall, perhaps the greatest of all the chief justices, the Supreme Court established an expansive view of the powers of the federal government and of the supremacy of national over state power.

Opinion of the Court by Chief Justice Marshall:

This government is acknowledged by all to be one of enumerated powers. The principle that it can exercise only the powers granted to it would seem too apparent to have required to be enforced by all those arguments, which its enlightened friends, while it was depending before the people, found it necessary to urge; that principle is now universally admitted. But the question respecting the extent of the powers actually granted is perpetually arising, and will probably continue to arise so long as our system shall exist. In discussing these questions, the conflicting powers of the general and state governments must be brought into view, and the supremacy of their respective laws, when they are in opposition, must be settled.

If any one proposition could command the universal assent of mankind, we might expect it would be this— that the government of the Union, though limited in its powers, is supreme within its sphere of action. This would seem to result necessarily from its nature. It is the government of all; its powers are delegated by all; it represents all, and acts for all. Though any one state may be willing to control its operations, no state is willing to allow others to control them. The nation, on those subjects on which it can act, must necessarily bind its component parts. But this question is not left to mere reason; the people have, in express terms, decided it by saying, "this Constitution, and the laws of the United States, which shall be made in pursuance thereof," "shall be the supreme law of the land," and by requiring that the members of the state legislatures and the officers of the executive and judicial departments of the states shall take the oath of fidelity to it. The government of the United States, then, though limited in its powers, is supreme, and its laws, when made in pursuance of the Constitution, form the supreme law of the land, "anything in the Constitution or laws of any state to the contrary notwithstanding."

The sword and the purse, all the external relations, and no inconsiderable portion of the industry of the nation, are intrusted to its government. It can never be pretended that these vast powers draw after them others of inferior importance merely because they are inferior. Such an idea can never be advanced. But it may with great reason be contended that a government intrusted with such ample powers, on the due execution of which the happiness and prosperity of the nation so vitally depends, must also be intrusted with ample means for their execution. The power being given, it is the interest of the nation to facilitate its execution. It can never be their interest, and cannot be presumed to have been their intention, to clog and embarrass its execution by withholding the most appropriate means. Throughout this vast republic, from the St. Croix to the Gulf of Mexico, from the Atlantic to the Pacific, revenue is to be collected and expended, armies are to be marched and supported. The exigencies of the nation may require that the treasure raised in the north should be transported to the south, that raised in the east, conveyed to the west, or that this order should be reversed. Is that construction of the Constitution to be preferred which would render these operations difficult, hazardous and expensive? Can we adopt that construction (unless the words imperiously require it) which would impute to the framers of that instrument, when granting these powers for the public good, the intention of impeding their exercise, by withholding a choice of means? If, indeed, such be the mandate of the Constitution, we have only to obey; but that instrument does not profess to enumerate the means by which the powers it confers may be executed; nor does it prohibit the creation of a corporation, if the existence of such a being be essential, to the beneficial exercise of those powers. It is, then, the subject of fair inquiry how far such means may be employed.

It is not denied that the powers given to the government imply the ordinary means of execution. The government which has a right to do an act and has imposed on it the duty of performing that act must, according to the dictates of reason, be allowed to select the means, and those who contend that it may not select any appropriate means that one particular mode of effecting the object is excepted take upon themselves the burden of establishing that exception.

But the argument on which most reliance is placed is drawn from that peculiar language of this clause. Congress is not empowered by it to make all laws which may have relation to the powers conferred on the government, but such only as may be "necessary and proper" for carrying them into execution. The word "necessary" is considered as controlling the whole sentence, and as limiting the right to pass laws for the execution of the granted powers to such as are indispensable, and without which the power would be nugatory. That it excludes the choice of means, and leaves to Congress in each case that only which is most direct and simple.

Is it true that this is the sense in which the word "necessary" is always used? Does it always import an absolute physical necessity so strong that one thing to which another may be termed necessary cannot exist without that other? We think it does not. If reference be had to its use in the common affairs of the world or in approved authors, we find that it frequently imports no more than that one thing is convenient, or useful, or essential to another. To employ the means necessary to an end is generally understood as employing any means calculated to produce the end, and not as being confined to those single means without which the end would be entirely unattainable. This word, then, like others, is used in various senses, and, in its construction, the subject, the context, the intention of the person using them are all to be taken into view.

Let this be done in the case under consideration. The subject is the execution of those great powers on which the welfare of a nation essentially depends. It must have been the intention of those who gave these powers to insure, so far as human prudence could insure, their beneficial execution. This could not be done by confiding the choice of means to such narrow limits as not to leave it in the power of Congress to adopt any which might be appropriate, and which were conducive to the end. This provision is made in a Constitution intended to endure for ages to come, and consequently to be adapted to the various crises of human affairs.

We admit, as all must admit, that the powers of the government are limited, and that its limits are not to be transcended. But we think the sound construction of the Constitution must allow to the national legislature that discretion with respect to the means by which the powers it confers are to be carried into execution which will enable that body to perform the high duties assigned to it in the manner most beneficial to the people. Let the end be legitimate, let it be within the scope of the Constitution, and all means which are appropriate, which are plainly adapted to that end, which are not prohibited, but consist with the letter and spirit of the Constitution, are constitutional.

The power of Congress to create and, of course, to continue the bank was the subject of the preceding part of this opinion, and is no longer to be considered as questionable. That the power of taxing it by the States may be exercised so as to destroy it is too obvious to be denied.

That the power to tax involves the power to destroy; that the power to destroy may defeat and render useless the power to create; that there is a plain repugnance in conferring on one government a power to control the constitutional measures of another, which other, with respect to those very measures, is declared to be supreme over that which exerts the control, are propositions not to be denied.

The Court has bestowed on this subject its most deliberate consideration. The result is a conviction that the states have no power, by taxation or otherwise, to retard, impede, burden, or in any manner control the operations of the constitutional laws enacted by Congress to carry into execution the powers vested in the general government. This is, we think, the unavoidable consequence of that supremacy which the Constitution has declared.

We are unanimously of opinion that the law passed by the Legislature of Maryland, imposing a tax on the Bank of the United States, is unconstitutional and void.

MARBURY V. MADISON, 5 U.S. 137 (1803)

The Constitution states that it is "the supreme law of the land." In the early Republic, the meaning of this Supremacy Clause was not clear. Nor was it clear who decides what the terms of the document mean and who enforces its commands. In 1803 the Supreme Court, in an opinion by Chief Justice John Marshall, reaffirmed the general principle that the Constitution trumps any other government action and resolved the issue of whose interpretation is final. In *Marbury v. Madison*, one of the seminal decisions in constitutional law, he held that because the Constitution is law, it is up to the courts, the law-interpreting and law-applying institution of government, to determine conclusively what the Constitution means and to require the other branches of government to adhere to the courts' interpretation. The Court's resolution has been contested from time to time (see the discussion of *Cooper v. Aaron* below), but judicial review has become a basic principle of American democracy.

Just before he left office in March of 1801, President John Adams made a number of last-minute judicial appointments in an attempt to retain control of the federal judiciary. When the new administration of Thomas Jefferson took office, James Madison, the new secretary of state, refused to formally deliver the commissions of the appointees. James Marbury, who had been appointed justice of the peace for the District of Columbia, sued to obtain his commission. The Supreme Court held that Marbury had a right to its commission, but the Court could not give him a remedy because the Judiciary Act giving the Court jurisdiction was an unconstitutional expansion of its powers. Although it limited the Court's authority in this case, the decision expanded its role by assigning to itself the power to determine the constitutionality of acts of Congress.

Opinion of the Court by Chief Justice Marshall:

The very essence of civil liberty certainly consists in the right of every individual to claim the protection of the laws whenever he receives an injury. One of the first duties of government is to afford that protection.

The Government of the United States has been emphatically termed a government of laws, and not of men. It will certainly cease to deserve this high appellation if the laws furnish no remedy for the violation of a vested legal right.

The question whether an act repugnant to the Constitution can become the law of the land is a question deeply interesting to the United States, but, happily, not of an intricacy proportioned to its interest. It seems only necessary to recognise certain principles, supposed to have been long and well established, to decide it.

That the people have an original right to establish for their future government such principles as, in their opinion, shall most conduce to their own happiness is the basis on which the whole American fabric has been erected. The exercise of this original right is a very great exertion; nor can it nor ought it to be frequently repeated. The principles, therefore, so established are deemed fundamental. And as the authority from which they proceed, is supreme, and can seldom act, they are designed to be permanent.

This original and supreme will organizes the government and assigns to different departments their respective powers. It may either stop here or establish certain limits not to be transcended by those departments.

The government of the United States is of the latter description. The powers of the legislature are defined and limited; and that those limits may not be mistaken or forgotten, the Constitution is written. To what purpose are powers limited, and to what purpose is that limitation committed to writing, if these limits may at any time be passed by those intended to be restrained? The distinction between a government with limited and unlimited powers is abolished if those limits do not confine the persons on whom they are imposed, and if acts prohibited and acts allowed are of equal obligation. It is a proposition too plain to be contested that the Constitution controls any legislative act repugnant to it, or that the legislature may alter the Constitution by an ordinary act.

Between these alternatives there is no middle ground. The Constitution is either a superior, paramount law, unchangeable by ordinary means, or it is on a level with ordinary legislative acts, and like other acts, is alterable when the legislature shall please to alter it.

If the former part of the alternative be true, then a legislative act contrary to the Constitution is not law;

if the latter part be true, then written constitutions are absurd attempts on the part of the people to limit a power in its own nature illimitable.

Certainly all those who have framed written constitutions contemplate them as forming the fundamental and paramount law of the nation, and consequently the theory of every such government must be that an act of the legislature repugnant to the Constitution is void.

This theory is essentially attached to a written Constitution, and is consequently to be considered by this Court as one of the fundamental principles of our society. It is not, therefore, to be lost sight of in the further consideration of this subject.

If an act of the legislature, repugnant to the Constitution is void, does it, notwithstanding its invalidity, bind the courts and oblige them to give it effect? Or, in other words, though it be not law, does it constitute a rule as operative as if it was a law? This would be to overthrow in fact what was established in theory, and would seem, at first view, an absurdity too gross to be insisted on. It shall, however, receive a more attentive consideration.

It is emphatically the province and duty of the judicial department to say what the law is. Those who apply the rule to particular cases must, of necessity, expound and interpret that rule. If two laws conflict with each other, the Courts must decide on the operation of each.

If, then, the courts are to regard the Constitution, and the Constitution is superior to any ordinary act of the legislature, the Constitution, and not such ordinary act, must govern the case to which they both apply.

Those, then, who controvert the principle that the Constitution is to be considered in court as a paramount law are reduced to the necessity of maintaining that courts must close their eyes on the Constitution, and see only the law.

This doctrine would subvert the very foundation of all written constitutions. It would declare that an act which, according to the principles and theory of our government, is entirely void, is yet, in practice, completely obligatory. It would declare that if the legislature shall do what is expressly forbidden, such act, notwithstanding the express prohibition, is in reality effectual. It would be giving to the legislature a practical and real omnipotence with the same breath which professes to restrict their powers within narrow limits. It is prescribing limits, and declaring that those limits may be passed as pleasure.

That it thus reduces to nothing what we have deemed the greatest improvement on political institutions—a written constitution—would of itself be sufficient, in America where written constitutions have been viewed with so much reverence, for rejecting the construction. But the peculiar expressions of the Constitution of the United States furnish additional arguments in favour of its rejection.

The judicial power of the United States is extended to all cases arising under the Constitution.

Could it be the intention of those who gave this power to say that, in using it, the Constitution should not be looked into? That a case arising under the Constitution should be decided without examining the instrument under which it arises? This is too extravagant to be maintained.

COOPER V. AARON, 358 U.S. 1 (1958)

Following the Supreme Court's decision in *Brown v. Board of Education* requiring schools to be desegregated (see chapter 4), many southern states resisted federal court orders desegregating their schools in compliance with the decision. In defiance of a court order, Arkansas governor Orval Faubus called out the National Guard and declared the Little Rock schools off limits to black students, a position that was thwarted when President Eisenhower ordered federal troops in to protect the students. The school board sought a postponement of the desegregation order because of the "chaos, bedlam, and turmoil" in the situation. The Supreme Court reversed the district court's grant of delay, asserting the supremacy of the federal court's application of constitutional rights. The Court signaled the importance of the decision by taking the unusual step of having each justice attach his name to the opinion individually, instead of simply stating that it was unanimous.

Opinion of the Court by Chief Justice Warren and Justices Black, Frankfurter, Douglas, Burton, Clark, Harlan, Brennan, and Whittaker:

The constitutional rights of respondents are not to be sacrificed or yielded to the violence and disorder which have followed upon the actions of the Governor and Legislature. As this Court said some 41 years ago in a unanimous opinion in a case involving another aspect of racial segregation: "It is urged that this proposed segregation will promote the public peace by preventing race conflicts. Desirable as this is, and important as is the preservation of the public peace, this aim cannot be accomplished by laws or ordinances which deny rights created or protected by the federal Constitution." Thus law and order are not here to be preserved by depriving the Negro children of their constitutional rights. The record before us clearly establishes that the growth of the Board's difficulties to a magnitude beyond its unaided power to control is the product of state action. Those difficulties, as counsel for the Board forthrightly conceded on the oral argument in this Court, can also be brought under control by state action.

The controlling legal principles are plain. The command of the Fourteenth Amendment is that no "State" shall deny to any person within its jurisdiction the equal protection of the laws. "A State acts by its legislative, its executive, or its judicial authorities. It can act in no other way. The constitutional provision, therefore, must mean that no agency of the State, or of the officers or agents by whom its powers are exerted, shall deny to any person within its jurisdiction the equal protection of the laws. Whoever, by virtue of public position under a State government, . . . denies or takes away the equal protection of the laws violates the constitutional inhibition; and as he acts in the name and for the State, and is clothed with the State's power, his act is that of the State. This must be so, or the constitutional prohibition has no meaning." Thus the prohibitions of the Fourteenth Amendment extend to all action of the State denying equal protection of the laws; whatever the agency of the State taking the action, or whatever the guise in which it is taken. In short, the constitutional rights of children not to be discriminated against in school admission on grounds of race or color declared by this Court in the *Brown* case can neither be nullified openly and directly by state legislators or state executive or judicial officers nor nullified indirectly by them through evasive schemes for segregation whether attempted "ingeniously or ingenuously."

What has been said, in the light of the facts developed, is enough to dispose of the case. However, we should answer the premise of the actions of the Governor and Legislature that they are not bound by our holding in the *Brown* case. It is necessary only to recall some basic constitutional propositions which are settled doctrine.

Article VI of the Constitution makes the Constitution the "supreme Law of the Land." In 1803, Chief Justice Marshall, speaking for a unanimous Court, referring to the Constitution as "the fundamental and paramount law of the nation," declared in the notable case of *Marbury v. Madison,* that "It is emphatically the province and duty of the judicial department to say what the law is." This decision declared the basic principle that the federal judiciary is supreme in the exposition of the law of the Constitution, and that principle has ever since been respected by this Court and the Country as a permanent and indispensable feature of our constitutional system. It follows that the interpretation of the Fourteenth Amendment enunciated by this Court in the *Brown* case is the supreme law of the land, and Article VI of the Constitution makes it of binding effect on the States "any Thing in the Constitution or Laws of any State to the Contrary notwithstanding." Every state legislator and executive and judicial officer is solemnly committed by oath taken pursuant to Article VI, clause 3 "to support this Constitution." Chief Justice Taney, speaking for a unanimous Court in 1859, said that this requirement reflected the framers' "anxiety to preserve it [the Constitution] in full force, in all its powers, and to guard against resistance to or evasion of its authority, on the part of a State. . . ."

No state legislator or executive or judicial officer can war against the Constitution without violating his undertaking to support it. Chief Justice Marshall spoke for a unanimous Court in saying that: "If the legislatures of the several states may, at will, annul the judgments of the courts of the United States, and destroy the rights acquired under those judgments, the Constitution itself becomes a solemn mockery." A Governor who asserts a power to nullify a federal court order is similarly restrained. If he had such power, said Chief Justice Hughes, in 1932, also for a unanimous Court, "it is manifest that the fiat of a state Governor, and not the Constitution of the United States, would be the supreme law of the land; that the restrictions of the Federal Constitution upon the exercise of state power would be but impotent phrases. . . ."

UNITED STATES V. NIXON, 418 U.S. 683 (1974)

When it became apparent that employees of President Richard Nixon's 1972 reelection committee had planned and participated in illegal acts, including a bungled burglary at the Watergate headquarters of the Democratic National Committee, a special prosecutor was appointed to investigate. After a grand jury indicted employees of the reelection committee and associates of President Nixon, the federal court in Washington, at the request of the special prosecutor, issued a subpoena to the president, demanding he turn over tape recordings of conversations with his advisers and other documents. President Nixon released edited transcripts of some of the tapes but moved to quash the subpoena, claiming the conversations and documents were protected by executive privilege. In an opinion by Chief Justice Warren Burger (who had been appointed by President Nixon), the Court reaffirmed its own supremacy in constitutional interpretation and denied the claim of executive privilege. The tapes were extremely damaging to the president because they showed his complicity in the illegal activities; as a result, when the Court ordered their production, his resignation under the threat of impeachment quickly followed.

Opinion of the Court by Chief Justice Burger:

[W]e turn to the claim that the subpoena should be quashed because it demands "confidential conversations between a President and his close advisors that it would be inconsistent with the public interest to produce." The first contention is a broad claim that the separation of powers doctrine precludes judicial review of a President's claim of privilege. The second contention is that, if he does not prevail on the claim of absolute privilege, the court should hold as a matter of constitutional law that the privilege prevails over the subpoena *duces tecum.*

In the performance of assigned constitutional duties, each branch of the Government must initially interpret the Constitution, and the interpretation of its powers by any branch is due great respect from the others. The President's counsel, as we have noted, reads the Constitution as providing an absolute privilege of confidentiality for all Presidential communications. Many decisions of this Court, however, have unequivocally reaffirmed the holding of *Marbury v. Madison* that "[i]t is emphatically the province and duty of the judicial department to say what the law is."

No holding of the Court has defined the scope of judicial power specifically relating to the enforcement of a subpoena for confidential Presidential communications for use in a criminal prosecution, but other exercises of power by the Executive Branch and the Legislative Branch have been found invalid as in conflict with the Constitution. Since this Court has consistently exercised the power to construe and delineate claims arising under express powers, it must follow that the Court has authority to interpret claims with respect to powers alleged to derive from enumerated powers.

Our system of government "requires that federal courts on occasion interpret the Constitution in a manner at variance with the construction given the document by another branch." In *Baker v. Carr*, 369 U.S. 186 (1962), the Court stated: "Deciding whether a matter has in any measure been committed by the Constitution to another branch of government, or whether the action of that branch exceeds whatever authority has been committed, is itself a delicate exercise in constitutional interpretation, and is a responsibility of this Court as ultimate interpreter of the Constitution."

Notwithstanding the deference each branch must accord the others, the "judicial Power of the United States" vested in the federal courts by Article III, section 1 of the Constitution can no more be shared with the Executive Branch than the Chief Executive, for example, can share with the Judiciary the veto power, or the Congress share with the Judiciary the power to override a Presidential veto. Any other conclusion would be contrary to the basic concept of separation of powers and the checks and balances that flow from the scheme of a tripartite government. We therefore reaffirm that it is the province and duty of this Court "to say what the law is" with respect to the claim of privilege presented in this case.

In support of his claim of absolute privilege, the President's counsel urges two grounds, one of which is common to all governments and one of which is peculiar to our system of separation of powers. The first ground is the valid need for protection of communications between high Government officials and those who advise and assist them in the performance of their manifold duties; the importance of this confidentiality is too plain to require further discussion. Human experience teaches that those who expect public dissemination of their remarks may well temper candor with a concern for appearances and for their own interests to the detriment of the decisionmaking process. Whatever the nature of the privilege of confidentiality of Presidential communications in the exercise of Article II powers, the privilege can be said to derive from the supremacy of each branch within its own assigned area of constitutional duties. Certain powers and privileges flow from the nature of enumerated powers; the protection of the confidentiality of Presidential communications has similar constitutional underpinnings.

The second ground asserted by the President's counsel in support of the claim of absolute privilege rests on the doctrine of separation of powers. Here it is argued that the independence of the Executive Branch within its own sphere insulates a President from a judicial subpoena in an ongoing criminal prosecution, and thereby protects confidential Presidential communications.

However, neither the doctrine of separation of powers nor the need for confidentiality of high-level communications, without more, can sustain an absolute, unqualified Presidential privilege of immunity from judicial process under all circumstances. The President's need for complete candor and objectivity from advisers calls for great deference from the courts. However, when the privilege depends solely on the broad, undifferentiated claim of public interest in the confidentiality of such conversations, a confrontation with other values arises. Absent a claim of need to protect military, diplomatic, or sensitive national security secrets, we find it difficult to accept the argument that even the very important interest in confidentiality of Presidential communications is significantly diminished by production of such material for *in camera* inspection with all the protection that a district court will be obliged to provide.

The impediment that an absolute, unqualified privilege would place in the way of the primary constitutional duty of the Judicial Branch to do justice in criminal prosecutions would plainly conflict with the function of the courts under Article III. In designing the structure of our Government and dividing and allocating the sovereign power among three co-equal branches, the Framers of the Constitution sought to provide a comprehensive system, but the separate powers were not intended to operate with absolute independence.

To read the Article II powers of the President as providing an absolute privilege as against a subpoena essential to enforcement of criminal statutes on no more than a generalized claim of the public interest in confidentiality of nonmilitary and nondiplomatic discussions would upset the constitutional balance of "a workable government" and gravely impair the role of the courts under Article III.

Since we conclude that the legitimate needs of the judicial process may outweigh Presidential privilege, it is necessary to resolve those competing interests in a manner that preserves the essential functions of each branch. The right and indeed the duty to resolve that question does not free the Judiciary from according high respect to the representations made on behalf of the President.

The expectation of a President to the confidentiality of his conversations and correspondence, like the claim of confidentiality of judicial deliberations, for example, has all the values to which we accord deference for the privacy of all citizens and, added to those values, is the necessity for protection of the public interest in candid, objective, and even blunt or harsh opinions in Presidential decisionmaking. A President and those who assist him must be free to explore alternatives in the process of shaping policies and making decisions, and to do so in a way many would be unwilling to express except privately. These are the considerations justifying a presumptive privilege for Presidential communications. The privilege is fundamental to the operation of Government, and inextricably rooted in the separation of powers under the Constitution.

But this presumptive privilege must be considered in light of our historic commitment to the rule of law. This is nowhere more profoundly manifest than, in our view, that "the twofold aim [of criminal justice] is that guilt shall not escape or innocence suffer." We have elected to employ an adversary system of criminal justice in which the parties contest all issues before a court of law. The need to develop all relevant facts in the adversary system is both fundamental and comprehensive. The ends of criminal justice would be defeated if judgments were to be founded on a partial or speculative presentation of the facts. The very integrity of the judicial system and public confidence in the system depend on full disclosure of all the facts, within the framework of the rules of evidence. To ensure that justice is done, it is imperative to the function of courts that compulsory process be available for the production of evidence needed either by the prosecution or by the defense.

Only recently the Court restated the ancient proposition of law, albeit in the context of a grand jury inquiry, rather than a trial, "that 'the public . . . has a right to every man's evidence,' except for those persons protected by a constitutional, common law, or statutory privilege."

In this case, the President challenges a subpoena served on him as a third party requiring the production of materials for use in a criminal prosecution; he does so on the claim that he has a privilege against disclosure of confidential communications.

In this case, we must weigh the importance of the general privilege of confidentiality of Presidential communications in performance of the President's responsibilities against the inroads of such a privilege on the fair administration of criminal justice. The interest in preserving confidentiality is weighty indeed, and entitled to great respect. However, we cannot conclude that advisers will be moved to temper the candor of their remarks by the infrequent occasions of disclosure because of the possibility that such conversations will be called for in the context of a criminal prosecution.

On the other hand, the allowance of the privilege to withhold evidence that is demonstrably relevant in a criminal trial would cut deeply into the guarantee of due process of law and gravely impair the basic function of the courts. A President's acknowledged need for confidentiality in the communications of his office is general in nature, whereas the constitutional need for production of relevant evidence in a criminal proceeding is specific and central to the fair adjudication of a particular criminal case in the administration of justice. Without access to specific facts, a criminal prosecution may be totally frustrated. The President's broad interest in confidentiality of communications will not be vitiated by disclosure of a limited number of conversations preliminarily shown to have some bearing on the pending criminal cases.

We conclude that, when the ground for asserting privilege as to subpoenaed materials sought for use in a criminal trial is based only on the generalized interest in confidentiality, it cannot prevail over the fundamental demands of due process of law in the fair administration of criminal justice. The generalized assertion of privilege must yield to the demonstrated, specific need for evidence in a pending criminal trial.

HAMDI V. RUMSFELD, 542 U.S. 507 (2004)

Following the terrorist attacks of September 11, 2001, Congress passed a resolution authorizing the president to use military force against the nations, persons, and organizations responsible for the attacks and to prevent future attacks. President George W. Bush ordered troops into Afghanistan to wage war against the Taliban government. In the course of that conflict, Yasir Hamdi, an American of Saudi descent, was captured and subsequently detained as an "enemy combatant" in naval brigs in the United States. Hamdi brought an action for habeas corpus, challenging whether he, an American citizen, could be indefinitely detained on American soil without the opportunity to challenge the basis for his detention. Habeas corpus, the "Great Writ," is the historic means of challenging unlawful detention by the government. The Supreme Court, in an opinion by Justice Sandra Day O'Connor, held that Hamdi had due process rights to receive notice of the basis for labeling him an enemy combatant and to contest that basis. Despite the president's role as commander in chief, the Court concluded that war did not give him "a blank check" to infringe the rights of American citizens.

Opinion of the Court by Justice O'Connor:

Even in cases in which the detention of enemy combatants is legally authorized, there remains the question of what process is constitutionally due to a citizen
who disputes his enemy-combatant status. Hamdi argues that he is owed a meaningful and timely hearing
and that "extra-judicial detention [that] begins and
ends with the submission of an affidavit based on
third-hand hearsay" does not comport with the Fifth
and Fourteenth Amendments. The Government coun-
ters that any more process than was provided below
would be both unworkable and "constitutionally intolerable." Our resolution of this dispute requires a careful
examination both of the writ of habeas corpus, which
Hamdi now seeks to employ as a mechanism of judicial
review, and of the Due Process Clause, which informs
the procedural contours of that mechanism in this instance.

Though they reach radically different conclusions on
the process that ought to attend the present proceeding, the parties begin on common ground. All agree
that, absent suspension, the writ of habeas corpus remains available to every individual detained within the
United States. U.S. Const., Art. I, § 9, cl. 2 ("The Privilege of the Writ of Habeas Corpus shall not be sus-
pended, unless when in Cases of Rebellion or Invasion
the public Safety may require it"). Only in the rarest of
circumstances has Congress seen fit to suspend the
writ. At all other times, it has remained a critical check
on the Executive, ensuring that it does not detain individuals except in accordance with law.

Both of these [the government's and Hamdi's] positions highlight legitimate concerns. And both empha-

size the tension that often exists between the autonomy that the Government asserts is necessary in order to pursue effectively a particular goal and the process that a citizen contends he is due before he is deprived of a constitutional right. The ordinary mechanism that we use for balancing such serious competing interests, and for determining the procedures that are necessary to ensure that a citizen is not "deprived of life, liberty, or property, without due process of law," U.S. Const., Amdt. 5, is the test that we articulated in *Mathews v. Eldridge,* 424 U.S. 319 (1976). *Mathews* dictates that the process due in any given instance is determined by weighing "the private interest that will be affected by the official action" against the Government's asserted interest, "including the function involved" and the burdens the Government would face in providing greater process. The *Mathews* calculus then contemplates a judicious balancing of these concerns, through an analysis of "the risk of an erroneous deprivation" of the private interest if the process were reduced and the "probable value, if any, of additional or substitute procedural safeguards." We take each of these steps in turn.

It is beyond question that substantial interests lie on both sides of the scale in this case. Hamdi's "private interest . . . affected by the official action," is the most elemental of liberty interests—the interest in being free from physical detention by one's own government. "We have always been careful not to 'minimize the importance and fundamental nature' of the individual's right to liberty," and we will not do so today.

Nor is the weight on this side of the *Mathews* scale offset by the circumstances of war or the accusation of treasonous behavior, for "[i]t is clear that commitment for *any* purpose constitutes a significant deprivation of liberty that requires due process protection." Moreover, as critical as the Government's interest may be in detaining those who actually pose an immediate threat to the national security of the United States during ongoing international conflict, history and common sense teach us that an unchecked system of detention carries the potential to become a means for oppression and abuse of others who do not present that sort of threat. We reaffirm today the fundamental nature of a citizen's right to be free from involuntary confinement by his own government without due process of law, and we weigh the opposing governmental interests against the curtailment of liberty that such confinement entails.

On the other side of the scale are the weighty and sensitive governmental interests in ensuring that those who have in fact fought with the enemy during a war do not return to battle against the United States. The law of war and the realities of combat may render such detentions both necessary and appropriate, and our due process analysis need not blink at those realities. Without doubt, our Constitution recognizes that core strategic matters of warmaking belong in the hands of those who are best positioned and most politically accountable for making them.

The Government also argues at some length that its interests in reducing the process available to alleged enemy combatants are heightened by the practical difficulties that would accompany a system of trial-like process. In its view, military officers who are engaged in the serious work of waging battle would be unnecessarily and dangerously distracted by litigation half a world away, and discovery into military operations would both intrude on the sensitive secrets of national defense and result in a futile search for evidence buried under the rubble of war. To the extent that these burdens are triggered by heightened procedures, they are properly taken into account in our due process analysis.

Striking the proper constitutional balance here is of great importance to the Nation during this period of ongoing combat. But it is equally vital that our calculus not give short shrift to the values that this country holds dear or to the privilege that is American citizenship. It is during our most challenging and uncertain moments that our Nation's commitment to due process is most severely tested; and it is in those times that we must preserve our commitment at home to the principles for which we fight abroad. "It would indeed be ironic if, in the name of national defense, we would sanction the subversion of one of those liberties . . . which makes the defense of the Nation worthwhile."

With due recognition of these competing concerns, we believe that neither the process proposed by the Government nor the process apparently envisioned by the District Court below strikes the proper constitutional balance when a United States citizen is detained in the United States as an enemy combatant. That is, "the risk of erroneous deprivation" of a detainee's liberty interest is unacceptably high under the Government's proposed rule, while some of the "additional or substitute procedural safeguards" suggested by the District Court are unwarranted in light of their limited "probable value" and the burdens they may impose on the military in such cases.

We therefore hold that a citizen-detainee seeking to challenge his classification as an enemy combatant

must receive notice of the factual basis for his classification, and a fair opportunity to rebut the Government's factual assertions before a neutral decisionmaker.
"For more than a century the central meaning of procedural due process has been clear: 'Parties whose
rights are to be affected are entitled to be heard; and in
order that they may enjoy that right they must first be
notified.' It is equally fundamental that the right to notice and an opportunity to be heard 'must be granted at
a meaningful time and in a meaningful manner.'" These
essential constitutional promises may not be eroded.

At the same time, the exigencies of the circumstances
may demand that, aside from these core elements, enemy
combatant proceedings may be tailored to alleviate their
uncommon potential to burden the Executive at a time of
ongoing military conflict. Hearsay, for example, may need
to be accepted as the most reliable available evidence
from the Government in such a proceeding. Likewise, the
Constitution would not be offended by a presumption in
favor of the Government's evidence, so long as that presumption remained a rebuttable one and fair opportunity
for rebuttal were provided. A burden-shifting scheme of
this sort would meet the goal of ensuring that the errant
tourist, embedded journalist, or local aid worker has a
chance to prove military error while giving due regard to
the Executive once it has put forth meaningful support
for its conclusion that the detainee is in fact an enemy
combatant. In the words of *Mathews*, process of this sort
would sufficiently address the "risk of an erroneous deprivation" of a detainee's liberty interest while eliminating
certain procedures that have questionable additional
value in light of the burden on the Government.

In so holding, we necessarily reject the Government's assertion that separation of powers principles mandate a heavily circumscribed role for the courts in such circumstances. Indeed, the position that the courts must forgo any examination of the individual case and focus exclusively on the legality of the broader detention scheme cannot be mandated by any reasonable view of separation of powers, as this approach serves only to *condense* power into a single branch of government. We have long since made clear that a state of war is not a blank check for the President when it comes to the rights of the Nation's citizens. Whatever power the United States Constitution envisions for the Executive in its exchanges with other nations or with enemy organizations in times of conflict, it most assuredly envisions a role for all three branches when individual liberties are at stake. The war power "is a power to wage war successfully, and thus it permits the harnessing of the entire energies of the people in a supreme cooperative effort to preserve the nation. But even the war power does not remove constitutional limitations safeguarding essential liberties." Likewise, we have made clear that, unless Congress acts to suspend it, the Great Writ of habeas corpus allows the Judicial Branch to play a necessary role in maintaining this delicate balance of governance, serving as an important judicial check on the Executive's discretion in the realm of detentions. Thus, while we do not question that our due process assessment must pay keen attention to the particular burdens faced by the Executive in the context of military action, it would turn our system of checks and balances on its head to suggest that a citizen could not make his way to court with a challenge to the factual basis for his detention by his government, simply because the Executive opposes making available such a challenge. Absent suspension of the writ by Congress, a citizen detained as an enemy combatant is entitled to this process.

Chapter 2

FREEDOM OF SPEECH

ABRAMS V. UNITED STATES, 250 U.S. 616 (1919)

Russian immigrants who described themselves as "revolutionists" and "anarchists" distributed leaflets in English and Yiddish in New York City advocating a general strike and calling on workers in weapons factories to stop producing material used by American troops against Russia. They were convicted under the 1918 amendments to the Espionage Act of 1917 for language "intended to incite, provoke and encourage resistance" to the war effort and to "urge, incite and advocate curtailment" of production for the war effort. The Supreme Court ruled, in an opinion by Justice John Clarke, that their conviction did not violate the First Amendment's guarantee of free speech.

In a majority opinion in an earlier case involving the Espionage Act, Justice Oliver Wendell Holmes Jr. had defined the test for constitutionality to be whether the words used in the circumstances presented "a clear and present danger that they will bring about the substantive evils that Congress has a right to prevent," *Schenck v. United States,* 249 U.S. 47 (1919). In that opinion he wrote the famous aphorism, "The most stringent protection of free speech would not protect a man in falsely shouting fire in a theatre and causing a panic." In *Abrams,* Holmes famously dissented from the application of the clear and present danger test to the "poor and puny anonymities" who distributed the leaflets and established the "marketplace of ideas" as a basis for First Amendment cases.

Opinion of the Court by Justice Clarke:

It will not do to say, as is now argued, that the only intent of these defendants was to prevent injury to the Russian cause. Men must be held to have intended, and to be accountable for, the effects which their acts were likely to produce. Even if their primary purpose and intent was to aid the cause of the Russian Revolution, the plan of action which they adopted necessarily involved, before it could be realized, defeat of the war program of the United States, for the obvious effect of this appeal, if it should become effective, as they hoped it might, would be to persuade persons of character such as those whom they regarded themselves as addressing, not to aid government loans, and not to work in ammunition factories where their work would produce "bullets, bayonets, cannon" and other munitions of war the use of which would cause the "murder" of Germans and Russians.

Justice Holmes, dissenting, joined by Justice Brandeis:

Persecution for the expression of opinions seems to me perfectly logical. If you have no doubt of your premises or your power, and want a certain result with all your heart, you naturally express your wishes in law, and sweep away all opposition. To allow opposition by speech seems to indicate that you think the speech impotent, as when a man says that he has squared the circle, or that you do not care wholeheartedly for the result, or that you doubt either your power or your premises. But when men have realized that time has upset many fighting faiths, they may come to believe even more than they believe the very foundations of their own conduct that the ultimate good desired is better reached by free trade in ideas—that the best test of truth is the power of the thought to get itself accepted in the competition of the market, and that truth is the only ground upon which their wishes safely can be carried out. That, at any rate, is the theory of our Constitution. It is an experiment, as all life is an experiment. Every year, if not every day, we have to wager our salvation upon some prophecy based upon imperfect knowledge. While that experiment is part of our system, I think that we should be eternally vigilant against attempts to check the expression of opinions that we loathe and believe to be fraught with death, unless they so imminently threaten immediate interference with the lawful and pressing purposes of the law that an immediate check is required to save the country. Only the emergency that makes it immediately dangerous to leave the correction of evil counsels to time warrants making any exception to the sweeping command, "Congress shall make no law . . . abridging the freedom of speech." Of course, I am speaking only of expressions of opinion and exhortations, which were all that were uttered here, but I regret that I cannot put into more impressive words my belief that, in their conviction upon this indictment, the defendants were deprived of their rights under the Constitution of the United States.

WHITNEY V. CALIFORNIA, 274 U.S. 357 (1927)

☞ Anita Whitney helped organize the Communist Labor Party of California. The party subscribed to the national party platform, which included "overthrow of the capitalist state" by "action of the masses." She was convicted under the California Syndicalism Act, which prohibited being a member of an organization that advocated unlawful methods as a means of bringing about socialism "or effecting any political change." Whitney argued that she and other party members had not intended to incite violence. A majority of the Court, in an opinion by Justice Terry Sanford, held that it was not a violation of the First Amendment to punish for words "tending to incite to crime," subsequently called the "bad tendency test." Justice Louis Brandeis, joined by Justice Holmes, concurred in the judgment because there was evidence of a conspiracy to commit crimes; his concurrence is a famous explanation of the important role of free speech.

In *Brandenburg v. Ohio*, 395 U.S. 444 (1969), the Court replaced the "clear and present danger" and "bad tendency" tests with a requirement that only "incite-

ment to imminent lawless action" could be punished
without violating the Free Speech Clause.

Justice Brandeis, joined by Justice Holmes, concurring:

Those who won our independence believed that the
final end of the State was to make men free to develop
their faculties, and that, in its government, the delib-
erative forces should prevail over the arbitrary. They
valued liberty both as an end, and as a means. They
believed liberty to be the secret of happiness, and cour-
age to be the secret of liberty. They believed that freedom to think as you will and to speak as you think are
means indispensable to the discovery and spread of
political truth; that, without free speech and assembly,
discussion would be futile; that, with them, discussion
affords ordinarily adequate protection against the dissemination of noxious doctrine; that the greatest men-
ace to freedom is an inert people; that public discussion
is a political duty, and that this should be a fundamental principle of the American government. They recognized the risks to which all human institutions are
subject. But they knew that order cannot be secured
merely through fear of punishment for its infraction;
that it is hazardous to discourage thought, hope and
imagination; that fear breeds repression; that repression breeds hate; that hate menaces stable government;
that the path of safety lies in the opportunity to discuss
freely supposed grievances and proposed remedies, and
that the fitting remedy for evil counsels is good ones.
Believing in the power of reason as applied through
public discussion, they eschewed silence coerced by

law—the argument of force in its worst form. Recognizing the occasional tyrannies of governing majorities, they amended the Constitution so that free speech and assembly should be guaranteed.

Fear of serious injury cannot alone justify suppression of free speech and assembly. Men feared witches and burnt women. It is the function of speech to free men from the bondage of irrational fears. To justify suppression of free speech, there must be reasonable ground to fear that serious evil will result if free speech is practiced. There must be reasonable ground to believe that the danger apprehended is imminent. There must be reasonable ground to believe that the evil to be prevented is a serious one.

Those who won our independence by revolution were not cowards. They did not fear political change. They did not exalt order at the cost of liberty. To courageous, self-reliant men, with confidence in the power of free and fearless reasoning applied through the processes of popular government, no danger flowing from speech can be deemed clear and present unless the incidence of the evil apprehended is so imminent that it may befall before there is opportunity for full discussion. If there be time to expose through discussion the falsehood and fallacies, to avert the evil by the processes of education, the remedy to be applied is more speech, not enforced silence. Only an emergency can justify repression. Such must be the rule if authority is to be reconciled with freedom. Such, in my opinion, is the command of the Constitution. It is therefore always open to Americans to challenge a law abridging free speech and assembly by showing that there was no emergency justifying it.

NEW YORK TIMES V. SULLIVAN, 376 U.S. 254 (1964)

In the midst of the civil rights struggle, a group called the Committee to Defend Martin Luther King and the Struggle for Freedom for the South purchased a full-page advertisement published in the *New York Times*. The advertisement alleged "a wave of terror" against nonviolent demonstrators, including the use of armed police at Alabama State College and multiple arrests and assaults of Dr. King. L. B. Sullivan, the police commissioner of Montgomery, Alabama, sued clergymen who had signed the advertisement and the *Times* under Alabama's libel law and was awarded damages of $500,000. The Supreme Court, in an opinion by Justice William Brennan, reversed the judgment for Sullivan, holding that actions for libel are subject to the First Amendment and that libel actions by public officials could succeed only if the official proved that the publication was made "with knowledge that it was false or with reckless disregard of whether it was false or not."

Opinion of the Court by Justice Brennan:

The general proposition that freedom of expression upon public questions is secured by the First Amendment has long been settled by our decisions. The constitutional safeguard, we have said, "was fashioned to assure unfettered interchange of ideas for the bringing about of political and social changes desired by the people." "The maintenance of the opportunity for free political discussion to the end that government may be responsive to the will of the people and that changes may be obtained by lawful means, an opportunity essential to the security of the Republic, is a fundamental principle of our constitutional system." "It is a prized American privilege to speak one's mind, although not always with perfect good taste, on all public institutions," and this opportunity is to be afforded for "vigorous advocacy" no less than "abstract discussion." The First Amendment, said Judge Learned Hand, "presupposes that right conclusions are more likely to be gathered out of a multitude of tongues than through any kind of authoritative selection. To many, this is, and always will be, folly, but we have staked upon it our all."

Thus, we consider this case against the background of a profound national commitment to the principle that debate on public issues should be uninhibited, robust, and wide-open, and that it may well include vehement, caustic, and sometimes unpleasantly sharp attacks on government and public officials.

The present advertisement, as an expression of grievance and protest on one of the major public issues of our time, would seem clearly to qualify for the constitutional protection. The question is whether it forfeits that protection by the falsity of some of its factual statements and by its alleged defamation of respondent.

Authoritative interpretations of the First Amendment guarantees have consistently refused to recognize an exception for any test of truth—whether administered by judges, juries, or administrative officials—and especially one that puts the burden of proving truth on the speaker. The constitutional protection does not turn upon "the truth, popularity, or social utility of the ideas and beliefs which are offered." As Madison said, "Some degree of abuse is inseparable from the proper use of every thing, and in no instance is this more true than in that of the press." In *Cantwell v. Connecticut,* 310 U.S. 296 (1940), the Court declared:

> In the realm of religious faith, and in that of political belief, sharp differences arise. In both fields, the tenets of one man may seem the rankest error to his neighbor. To persuade others to his own point of view, the pleader, as we know, at times resorts to exaggeration, to vilification of men who have been, or are, prominent in church or state, and even to false statement. But the people of this nation have ordained, in the light of history, that, in spite of the probability of excesses and abuses, these liberties are, in the long view, essential to enlightened opinion and right conduct on the part of the citizens of a democracy.

Erroneous statement is inevitable in free debate, and it must be protected if the freedoms of expression are to have the "breathing space" that they "need . . . to survive."

This is the lesson to be drawn from the great controversy over the Sedition Act of 1798, which first crystallized a national awareness of the central meaning of the First Amendment. That statute made it a crime, punishable by a $5,000 fine and five years in prison, "if any person shall write, print, utter or publish . . . any false, scandalous and malicious writing or writings against the government of the United States, or either house of the Congress . . . or the President . . . with intent to defame . . . or to bring them, or either of them, into contempt or disrepute; or to excite against them, or either or any of them, the hatred of the good people of the United States." The Act allowed the defendant the defense of truth, and provided that the jury were to be judges both of the law and the facts. Despite these qualifications, the Act was vigorously condemned as unconstitutional in an attack joined in by Jefferson and Madison.

Madison prepared the Report in support of the protest. His premise was that the Constitution created a form of government under which "The people, not the government, possess the absolute sovereignty." The structure of the government dispersed power in reflection of the people's distrust of concentrated power, and of power itself at all levels. This form of government was "altogether different" from the British form, under which the Crown was sovereign and the people were subjects. "Is it not natural and necessary, under such different circumstances," he asked, "that a different degree of freedom in the use of the press should be contemplated?" Earlier, in a debate in the House of Representatives, Madison had said: "If we advert to the nature of Republican Government, we shall find that the censorial power is in the people over the Government, and not in the Government over the people." The right of free public discussion of the stewardship of public officials was thus, in Madison's view, a fundamental principle of the American form of government.

Although the Sedition Act was never tested in this Court, the attack upon its validity has carried the day in the court of history. Fines levied in its prosecution were repaid by Act of Congress on the ground that it was unconstitutional. Jefferson, as President, pardoned those who had been convicted and sentenced under the

Act and remitted their fines. The invalidity of the Act has also been assumed by Justices of this Court. These views reflect a broad consensus that the Act, because of the restraint it imposed upon criticism of government and public officials, was inconsistent with the First Amendment.

What a State may not constitutionally bring about by means of a criminal statute is likewise beyond the reach of its civil law of libel. The fear of damage awards under a rule such as that invoked by the Alabama courts here may be markedly more inhibiting than the fear of prosecution under a criminal statute. The judgment awarded in this case—without the need for any proof of actual pecuniary loss—was one thousand times greater than the maximum fine provided by the Alabama [statute for criminal libel], and one hundred times greater than that provided by the Sedition Act. And since there is no double jeopardy limitation applicable to civil lawsuits, this is not the only judgment that may be awarded against petitioners for the same publication. Whether or not a newspaper can survive a succession of such judgments, the pall of fear and timidity imposed upon those who would give voice to public criticism is an atmosphere in which the First Amendment freedoms cannot survive.

CITIZENS UNITED V. FEDERAL ELECTION COMMISSION, 558 U.S. (2010)

Citizens United was a conservative, nonprofit organization that produced a documentary film *Hillary: The*

Movie, which was critical of presidential candidate Hillary Clinton. The group sought to advertise its movie on television and air the film on DirecTV. The advertisement and airing were held to violate the Bipartisan Campaign Reform Act (the McCain-Feingold Act), which limited the ability of corporations and unions to broadcast election-related materials shortly before Election Day. In an opinion by Justice Anthony Kennedy, the Court struck down portions of the law as restricting the First Amendment rights of corporations.

Opinion of the Court by Justice Kennedy:

The First Amendment provides that "Congress shall make no law . . . abridging the freedom of speech." Laws enacted to control or suppress speech may operate at different points in the speech process.

The law before us is an outright ban, backed by criminal sanctions. Section 441b makes it a felony for all corporations—including nonprofit advocacy corporations—either to expressly advocate the election or defeat of candidates or to broadcast electioneering communications within 30 days of a primary election and 60 days of a general election.

Section 441b's prohibition on corporate independent expenditures is thus a ban on speech. As a "restriction on the amount of money a person or group can spend on political communication during a campaign," that statute "necessarily reduces the quantity of expression by restricting the number of issues discussed, the depth of their exploration, and the size of the audience reached." Were the Court to uphold these restrictions, the Government could repress speech by silencing certain voices at any of the various points in the speech process.

Speech is an essential mechanism of democracy, for it is the means to hold officials accountable to the people. The right of citizens to inquire, to hear, to speak, and to use information to reach consensus is a precondition to enlightened self-government and a necessary means to protect it. The First Amendment "has its fullest and most urgent application" to speech uttered during a campaign for political office.

For these reasons, political speech must prevail against laws that would suppress it, whether by design or inadvertence. Laws that burden political speech are "subject to strict scrutiny," which requires the Government to prove that the restriction "furthers a compelling interest and is narrowly tailored to achieve that interest."

Quite apart from the purpose or effect of regulating content, moreover, the Government may commit a constitutional wrong when by law it identifies certain preferred speakers. By taking the right to speak from some and giving it to others, the Government deprives the disadvantaged person or class of the right to use speech to strive to establish worth, standing, and respect for the speaker's voice. The Government may not by these means deprive the public of the right and privilege to determine for itself what speech and speakers are worthy of consideration. The First Amendment protects speech and speaker, and the ideas that flow from each.

Political speech is "indispensable to decisionmaking in a democracy, and this is no less true because the speech comes from a corporation rather than an individual." The concept that government may restrict the speech of some elements of our society in order to enhance the relative voice of others is wholly foreign to the First Amendment.

It is irrelevant for purposes of the First Amendment that corporate funds may "have little or no correlation to the public's support for the corporation's political ideas." All speakers, including individuals and the media, use money amassed from the economic marketplace to fund their speech. The First Amendment protects the resulting speech, even if it was enabled by economic transactions with persons or entities who disagree with the speaker's ideas.

The Framers may not have anticipated modern business and media corporations. Yet television networks and major newspapers owned by media corporations have become the most important means of mass communication in modern times. The First Amendment was certainly not understood to condone the suppression of political speech in society's most salient media. It was understood as a response to the repression of speech and the press that had existed in England and the heavy taxes on the press that were imposed in the colonies. The great debates between the Federalists and the Anti-Federalists over our founding document were published and expressed in the most important means of mass communication of that era—newspapers owned by individuals. At the founding, speech was open, comprehensive, and vital to society's definition of itself; there were no limits on the sources of speech and knowledge. The Framers may have been unaware of certain types of speakers or forms of communication, but that does not mean that those speakers and media are entitled to less First Amendment protection than those types of speakers and media that provided the means of communicating political ideas when the Bill of Rights was adopted.

TEXAS V. JOHNSON, 491 U.S. 397 (1989)

While the 1984 Republican National Convention was taking place in Dallas, Gregory Lee Johnson participated in a protest that culminated when Johnson unfurled an American flag, doused it with kerosene, and set it on fire. While the flag burned, protesters chanted "America, the red, white, and blue, we spit on you." Johnson was charged with "desecration of a venerated object," convicted, and sentenced to one year in prison and a fine of $2,000.

The Supreme Court overturned the conviction in an opinion by Justice Brennan. The Court followed a long line of cases holding that the First Amendment's protection of "speech" included protection of conduct that expressed ideas and that, despite the American flag's unique role in national life, it did not have a special constitutional status. Chief Justice William Rehnquist, joined by Justices Byron White and Sandra Day O'Connor, dissented, arguing that the flag is a unique national symbol that deserves special protection.

Opinion of the Court by Justice Brennan:

The First Amendment literally forbids the abridgment only of "speech," but we have long recognized that its protection does not end at the spoken or written word. While we have rejected "the view that an apparently limitless variety of conduct can be labeled 'speech' whenever the person engaging in the conduct intends thereby to express an idea," we have acknowledged that conduct may be "sufficiently imbued with elements of communication to fall within the scope of the First and Fourteenth Amendments."

In deciding whether particular conduct possesses sufficient communicative elements to bring the First Amendment into play, we have asked whether "[a]n intent to convey a particularized message was present, and [whether] the likelihood was great that the message would be understood by those who viewed it."

Whether Johnson's treatment of the flag violated Texas law thus depended on the likely communicative impact of his expressive conduct.

We must therefore subject the State's asserted interest in preserving the special symbolic character of the flag to "the most exacting scrutiny."

Texas argues that its interest in preserving the flag as a symbol of nationhood and national unity survives this close analysis. Quoting extensively from the writings of this Court chronicling the flag's historic and symbolic role in our society, the State emphasizes the "special place" reserved for the flag in our Nation. The State's argument is not that it has an interest simply in maintaining the flag as a symbol of *something*, no matter what it symbolizes; indeed, if that were the State's position, it would be difficult to see how that interest is endangered by highly symbolic conduct such as Johnson's. Rather, the State's claim is that it has an interest in preserving the flag as a symbol of *nationhood* and *national unity,* a symbol with a determinate range of meanings. According to Texas, if one physically treats the flag in a way that would tend to cast doubt on either the idea that nationhood and national unity are the flag's referents or that national unity actually exists, the message conveyed thereby is a harmful one, and therefore may be prohibited.

If there is a bedrock principle underlying the First Amendment, it is that the government may not prohibit the expression of an idea simply because society finds the idea itself offensive or disagreeable.

We have not recognized an exception to this principle even where our flag has been involved. In holding in [*West Virginia State Board of Education v. Barnette,* 319 U.S. 624 (1943)] that the Constitution did not leave this course open to the government, Justice Jackson described one of our society's defining principles in words deserving of their frequent repetition:

> If there is any fixed star in our constitutional constellation, it is that no official, high or petty, can prescribe what shall be orthodox in politics, nationalism, religion, or other matters of opinion or force citizens to confess by word or act their faith therein.

Texas' focus on the precise nature of Johnson's expression, moreover, misses the point of our prior decisions: their enduring lesson, that the government may not prohibit expression simply because it disagrees with its message, is not dependent on the particular mode in which one chooses to express an idea. If we were to hold that a State may forbid flag burning wherever it is likely to endanger the flag's symbolic role, but allow it wherever burning a flag promotes that role—as where, for example, a person ceremoniously burns a dirty flag—we would be saying that when it comes to impairing the flag's physical integrity, the flag itself may be used as a symbol—as a substitute for the written or spoken word or a "short cut from mind to mind"—only in one direction. We would be permitting a State to "prescribe what shall be orthodox" by saying that one may burn the flag to convey one's attitude toward it and its referents only if one does not endanger the flag's representation of nationhood and national unity.

We are tempted to say, in fact, that the flag's deservedly cherished place in our community will be strengthened, not weakened, by our holding today. Our decision is a reaffirmation of the principles of freedom and inclusiveness that the flag best reflects, and of the conviction that our toleration of criticism such as Johnson's is a sign and source of our strength. Indeed, one of the proudest images of our flag, the one immortalized in our own national anthem, is of the bombardment it survived at Fort McHenry. It is the Nation's resilience, not its rigidity, that Texas sees reflected in the flag— and it is that resilience that we reassert today.

The way to preserve the flag's special role is not to punish those who feel differently about these matters. It is to persuade them that they are wrong.

And, precisely because it is our flag that is involved, one's response to the flag-burner may exploit the uniquely persuasive power of the flag itself. We can imagine no more appropriate response to burning a flag than waving one's own, no better way to counter a flag-burner's message than by saluting the flag that burns, no surer means of preserving the dignity even of the flag that burned than by—as one witness here did—according its remains a respectful burial. We do not consecrate the flag by punishing its desecration, for in doing so we dilute the freedom that this cherished emblem represents.

Chief Justice Rehnquist, dissenting:

In holding this Texas statute unconstitutional, the Court ignores Justice Holmes' familiar aphorism that "a page of history is worth a volume of logic." For more than 200 years, the American flag has occupied a unique position as the symbol of our Nation, a uniqueness that justifies a governmental prohibition against flag burning in the way respondent Johnson did here.

The American flag, then, throughout more than 200 years of our history, has come to be the visible symbol embodying our Nation. It does not represent the views of any particular political party, and it does not represent any particular political philosophy. The flag is not simply another "idea" or "point of view" competing for recognition in the marketplace of ideas. Millions and millions of Americans regard it with an almost mystical reverence, regardless of what sort of social, political, or philosophical beliefs they may have. I cannot agree that the First Amendment invalidates the Act of Congress, and the laws of 48 of the 50 States, which make criminal the public burning of the flag.

The public burning of the American flag by Johnson

was no essential part of any exposition of ideas, and at the same time it had a tendency to incite a breach of the peace.

Far from being a case of "one picture being worth a thousand words," flag burning is the equivalent of an inarticulate grunt or roar that, it seems fair to say, is most likely to be indulged in not to express any particular idea, but to antagonize others. Only five years ago we said in *City Council of Los Angeles v. Taxpayers for Vincent*, 466 U.S. 789 (1984), that "the First Amendment does not guarantee the right to employ every conceivable method of communication at all times and in all places." The Texas statute deprived Johnson of only one rather inarticulate symbolic form of protest—a form of protest that was profoundly offensive to many—and left him with a full panoply of other symbols and every conceivable form of verbal expression to express his deep disapproval of national policy. Thus, in no way can it be said that Texas is punishing him because his hearers—or any other group of people—were profoundly opposed to the message that he sought to convey. Such opposition is no proper basis for restricting speech or expression under the First Amendment. It was Johnson's use of this particular symbol, and not the idea that he sought to convey by it or by his many other expressions, for which he was punished.

Our Constitution wisely places limits on powers of legislative majorities to act, but the declaration of such limits by this Court "is, at all times, a question of much delicacy, which ought seldom, if ever, to be decided in the affirmative, in a doubtful case." Uncritical extension of constitutional protection to the burning of the flag risks the frustration of the very purpose for which organized governments are instituted. The Court decides that the

American flag is just another symbol, about which not only must opinions pro and con be tolerated, but for which the most minimal public respect may not be enjoined. The government may conscript men into the Armed Forces where they must fight and perhaps die for the flag, but the government may not prohibit the public burning of the banner under which they fight. I would uphold the Texas statute as applied in this case.

WEST VIRGINIA STATE BOARD OF EDUCATION V. BARNETTE, 319 U.S. 624 (1943)

☞ In 1942, the West Virginia State Board of Education adopted a rule requiring all teachers and students to say the Pledge of Allegiance to the flag. The Barnettes were Jehovah's Witnesses who believed that the Pledge of Allegiance violated the biblical prohibition on worshipping "graven images." They challenged the rule, arguing that it violated the constitutional protections of freedom of speech and freedom of religion. The Court, in an opinion by Justice Robert Jackson, agreed. The case illustrates that the First Amendment protects against compelled speech—the flag salute—as well as restrictions on speech.

Opinion of the Court by Justice Jackson:

As the present Chief Justice said in dissent in [*Minersville School District v. Gobitis*, 310 U.S. 586 (1940)], the State may "require teaching by instruction and study of all in our history and in the structure and organization of our government, including the guaranties of civil liberty, which tend to inspire patriotism and love of country." Here, however, we are dealing with a compulsion of students to declare a belief. They are not merely made acquainted with the flag salute so that they may be informed as to what it is or even what it means. The issue here is whether this slow and easily neglected route to aroused loyalties constitutionally may be short-cut by substituting a compulsory salute and slogan.

There is no doubt that, in connection with the pledges, the flag salute is a form of utterance. Symbolism is a primitive but effective way of communicating ideas. The use of an emblem or flag to symbolize some system, idea, institution, or personality is a short-cut from mind to mind. Causes and nations, political parties, lodges, and ecclesiastical groups seek to knit the loyalty of their followings to a flag or banner, a color or design. The State announces rank, function, and authority through crowns and maces, uniforms and black robes; the church speaks through the Cross, the Crucifix, the altar and shrine, and clerical raiment. Symbols of State often convey political ideas, just as religious symbols come to convey theological ones. Associated with many of these symbols are appropriate gestures of acceptance or respect: a salute, a bowed or bared head, a bended knee. A person gets from a symbol the meaning he puts into it, and what is one man's comfort and inspiration is another's jest and scorn.

Government of limited power need not be anemic government. Assurance that rights are secure tends to diminish fear and jealousy of strong government, and, by making us feel safe to live under it, makes for its better support. Without promise of a limiting Bill of Rights, it is doubtful if our Constitution could have mustered enough strength to enable its ratification. To enforce those rights today is not to choose weak government over strong government. It is only to adhere as a means of strength to individual freedom of mind in preference to officially disciplined uniformity for which history indicates a disappointing and disastrous end.

The very purpose of a Bill of Rights was to withdraw certain subjects from the vicissitudes of political controversy, to place them beyond the reach of majorities and officials, and to establish them as legal principles to be applied by the courts. One's right to life, liberty, and property, to free speech, a free press, freedom of worship and assembly, and other fundamental rights may not be submitted to vote; they depend on the outcome of no elections.

Struggles to coerce uniformity of sentiment in support of some end thought essential to their time and country have been waged by many good, as well as by evil, men. Nationalism is a relatively recent phenomenon, but, at other times and places, the ends have been racial or territorial security, support of a dynasty or regime, and particular plans for saving souls. As first and moderate methods to attain unity have failed, those bent on its accomplishment must resort to an ever-increasing severity. As governmental pressure toward unity becomes greater, so strife becomes more bitter as to whose unity it shall be. Probably no deeper division of our people could proceed from any provocation than from finding it necessary to choose what doctrine and whose program public educational officials shall compel youth to unite in embracing. Ultimate futility of such attempts to compel coherence is the lesson of every such effort from the Roman drive to stamp out Christianity as a disturber of its pagan unity, the Inquisition, as a means to religious and dynastic unity, the Siberian exiles as a means to Russian unity, down to the fast failing efforts of our present totalitarian enemies. Those who begin coercive elimination of dissent soon find themselves exterminating dissenters. Compulsory unification of opinion achieves only the unanimity of the graveyard.

It seems trite but necessary to say that the First Amendment to our Constitution was designed to avoid these ends by avoiding these beginnings. There is no mysticism in the American concept of the State or of the nature or origin of its authority. We set up government by consent of the governed, and the Bill of Rights denies those in power any legal opportunity to coerce that consent. Authority here is to be controlled by public opinion, not public opinion by authority.

The case is made difficult not because the principles of its decision are obscure, but because the flag involved is our own. Nevertheless, we apply the limitations of the Constitution with no fear that freedom to be intellectually and spiritually diverse or even contrary will disintegrate the social organization. To believe that patriotism will not flourish if patriotic ceremonies are voluntary and spontaneous, instead of a compulsory routine, is to make an unflattering estimate of the appeal of our institutions to free minds. We can have intellectual individualism and the rich cultural diversities that we owe to exceptional minds only at the price of occasional eccentricity and abnormal attitudes. When they are so harmless to others or to the State as those we deal with here, the price is not too great. But freedom to differ is not limited to things that do not matter much. That would be a mere shadow of freedom. The test of its substance is the right to differ as to things that touch the heart of the existing order.

If there is any fixed star in our constitutional constellation, it is that no official, high or petty, can prescribe what shall be orthodox in politics, nationalism, religion, or other matters of opinion, or force citizens to confess by word or act their faith therein. If there are any circumstances which permit an exception, they do not now occur to us.

We think the action of the local authorities in compelling the flag salute and pledge transcends constitutional limitations on their power, and invades the sphere of intellect and spirit which it is the purpose of the First Amendment to our Constitution to reserve from all official control.

BOY SCOUTS OF AMERICA V. DALE, 530 U.S. 640 (2000)

James Dale joined the Cub Scouts when he was eight years old, became an Eagle Scout, and, as an adult, an assistant scoutmaster. While at college he joined the Rutgers University Lesbian/Gay Alliance and gave a newspaper interview about the need of gay teenagers for role models. He then received a letter from the executive of the local Scout council revoking his adult membership because the Boy Scouts "specifically forbid membership to homosexuals." Dale filed a complaint under the New Jersey law that prohibited discrimination on the basis of sexual orientation. The Supreme Court, in an opinion by Chief Justice William Rehnquist, upheld Dale's dismissal. The Court concluded that the New Jersey law violated the right of association inherent in the First Amendment and that the Scouts' position on homosexuality was a form of protected expression.

Opinion of the Court by Chief Justice Rehnquist:

In *Roberts v. United States Jaycees*, 468 U.S. 609 (1984), we observed that "implicit in the right to engage in activities protected by the First Amendment" is "a corresponding right to associate with others in pursuit of a wide variety of political, social, economic, educational, religious, and cultural ends." This right is crucial in preventing the majority from imposing its views on groups that would rather express other, perhaps unpopular, ideas. Government actions that may unconstitutionally burden this freedom may take many forms, one of which is "intrusion into the internal structure or affairs of an association" like a "regulation that forces the group to accept members it does not desire." Forcing a group to accept certain members may impair the ability of the group to express those views, and only those views, that it intends to express. Thus, "freedom of association . . . plainly presupposes a freedom not to associate."

The forced inclusion of an unwanted person in a group infringes the group's freedom of expressive association if the presence of that person affects in a significant way the group's ability to advocate public or private viewpoints. But the freedom of expressive association, like many freedoms, is not absolute. We have held that the freedom could be overridden "by regulations adopted to serve compelling state interests, unrelated to the suppression of ideas, that cannot be achieved through means significantly less restrictive of associational freedoms."

To determine whether a group is protected by the First Amendment's expressive associational right, we must determine whether the group engages in "expressive association." The First Amendment's protection of expressive association is not reserved for advocacy groups. But to come within its ambit, a group must engage in some form of expression, whether it be public or private.

The Boy Scouts is a private, nonprofit organization. According to its mission statement:

> It is the mission of the Boy Scouts of America to serve others by helping to instill values in young people and, in other ways, to prepare them to make ethical choices over their lifetime in achieving their full potential.
>
> The values we strive to instill are based on those found in the Scout Oath and Law:

> SCOUT OATH
> *On my honor I will do my best*
> *To do my duty to God and my country*
> *and to obey the Scout Law;*
> *To help other people at all times;*
> *To keep myself physically strong,*
> *mentally awake, and morally straight.*

The general mission of the Boy Scouts is clear: "[T]o instill values in young people." The Boy Scouts seeks to instill these values by having its adult leaders spend time with the youth members, instructing and engaging them in activities like camping, archery, and fishing. During the time spent with the youth members, the scoutmasters and assistant scoutmasters inculcate them with the Boy Scouts' values—both expressly and by example. It seems indisputable that an association that seeks to transmit such a system of values engages in expressive activity.

Given that the Boy Scouts engages in expressive activity, we must determine whether the forced inclusion of Dale as an assistant scoutmaster would significantly affect the Boy Scouts' ability to advocate public or private viewpoints. This inquiry necessarily requires us first to explore, to a limited extent, the nature of the Boy Scouts' view of homosexuality.

The values the Boy Scouts seeks to instill are "based on" those listed in the Scout Oath and Law. The Boy Scouts explains that the Scout Oath and Law provide "a positive moral code for living; they are a list of 'do's' rather than 'don'ts.'" The Boy Scouts asserts that homosexual conduct is inconsistent with the values embodied in the Scout Oath and Law, particularly with the values represented by the terms "morally straight" and "clean."

The Boy Scouts believes that homosexual conduct is inconsistent with the values it seeks to instill in its youth members; it will not "promote homosexual conduct as a legitimate form of behavior." The presence of Dale as an assistant scoutmaster would surely interfere with the Boy Scouts' choice not to propound a point of view contrary to its beliefs.

In speaking of the Founders of this Nation, Justice Brandeis emphasized that they "believed that the freedom to think as you will and to speak as you think are means indispensable to the discovery and spread of political truth." He continued: "Believing in the power of reason as applied through public discussion, they eschewed silence coerced by law—the argument of force in its worst form. Recognizing the occasional tyrannies of governing majorities, they amended the Constitution so that free speech and assembly should be guaranteed."

We are not, as we must not be, guided by our views of whether the Boy Scouts' teachings with respect to homosexual conduct are right or wrong; public or judicial disapproval of a tenet of an organization's expression does not justify the State's effort to compel the organization to accept members where such acceptance would derogate from the organization's expressive message. "While the law is free to promote all sorts of conduct in place of harmful behavior, it is not free to interfere with speech for no better reason than promoting an approved message or discouraging a disfavored one, however enlightened either purpose may strike the government."

Chapter 3

FREEDOM OF
RELIGION

EVERSON V. BOARD OF EDUCATION, 330 U.S. 1 (1947)

☞ A New Jersey school board authorized reimbursement to parents who used public buses to transport their children to school, including children attending public schools and Roman Catholic parochial schools. A taxpayer challenged the payment to the parents of parochial school students as violating the Establishment Clause of the First Amendment. The Supreme Court, in an opinion by Justice Hugo Black, upheld the reimbursements as a neutral measure not establishing a religion. In doing so, the Court rehearsed the history of the religion clauses and established the principle of a "wall of separation" between church and state.

Opinion of the Court by Justice Black:

The New Jersey statute is challenged as a "law respecting an establishment of religion." The First Amendment, as made applicable to the states by the Fourteenth, commands that a state "shall make no law respecting an establishment of religion, or prohibiting the free exercise thereof." These words of the First Amendment reflected in the minds of early Americans a vivid mental picture of conditions and practices which they fervently wished to stamp out in order to preserve liberty for themselves and for their posterity. Doubtless their goal has not been entirely reached; but so far has the Nation moved toward it that the expression "law respecting an establishment of religion" probably does not so vividly remind present-day Americans of the evils, fears, and political problems that caused that expression to be written into our Bill of Rights. Whether this New Jersey law is one respecting the "establishment of religion" requires an understanding of the meaning of that language, particularly with respect to the imposition of taxes. Once again, therefore, it is not inappropriate briefly to review the background and environment of the period in which that constitutional language was fashioned and adopted.

A large proportion of the early settlers of this country came here from Europe to escape the bondage of laws which compelled them to support and attend government-favored churches. The centuries immediately before and contemporaneous with the colonization of America had been filled with turmoil, civil strife, and persecutions, generated in large part by established sects determined to maintain their absolute political and religious supremacy. With the power of government supporting them, at various times and places, Catholics had persecuted Protestants, Protestants had persecuted Catholics, Protestant sects had persecuted other Protestant sects, Catholics of one shade of belief had persecuted Catholics of another shade of belief, and all of these had from time to time persecuted Jews. In efforts to force loyalty to whatever religious group happened to be on top and in league with the government of a particular time and place, men and women had been fined, cast in jail, cruelly tortured, and killed. Among the offenses for which these punishments had been inflicted were such things as speaking disrespectfully of the views of ministers of government-established churches, non-attendance at those churches, expressions of nonbelief in their doctrines, and failure to pay taxes and tithes to support them.

These practices of the old world were transplanted to and began to thrive in the soil of the new America. The very charters granted by the English Crown to the individuals and companies designated to make the laws which would control the destinies of the colonials authorized these individuals and companies to erect religious establishments which all, whether believers or nonbelievers, would be required to support and attend. An exercise of this authority was accompanied by a repetition of many of the old-world practices and persecutions. Catholics found themselves hounded and proscribed because of their faith; Quakers who followed their conscience went to jail; Baptists were peculiarly obnoxious to certain dominant Protestant sects; men and women of varied faiths who happened to be in a minority in a particular locality were persecuted because they steadfastly persisted in worshipping God only as their own consciences dictated. And all of these dissenters were compelled to pay tithes and taxes to support government-sponsored churches whose ministers preached inflammatory sermons designed to strengthen and consolidate the established faith by generating a burning hatred against dissenters.

These practices became so commonplace as to shock the freedom-loving colonials into a feeling of abhorrence. The imposition of taxes to pay ministers' salaries and to build and maintain churches and church property aroused their indignation. It was these feelings which found expression in the First Amendment. No one locality and no one group throughout the Colonies can rightly be given entire credit for having aroused the sentiment that culminated in adoption of the Bill of Rights' provisions embracing religious liberty. But Virginia, where the established church had achieved a dominant influence in political affairs and where many excesses attracted wide public attention, provided a great stimulus and able leadership for the movement. The people there, as elsewhere, reached the conviction that individual religious liberty could be achieved best under a government which was stripped of all power to tax, to support, or otherwise to assist any or all religions, or to interfere with the beliefs of any religious individual or group.

The movement toward this end reached its dramatic climax in Virginia in 1785–86 when the Virginia legislative body was about to renew Virginia's tax levy for the support of the established church. Thomas Jefferson and James Madison led the fight against this tax. Madison wrote his great Memorial and Remonstrance against the law. In it, he eloquently argued that a true religion did not need the support of law; that no person, either believer or nonbeliever, should be taxed to support a religious institution of any kind; that the best interest of a society required that the minds of men always be wholly free; and that cruel persecutions were the inevitable result of government-established religions. Madison's Remonstrance received strong support throughout Virginia, and the Assembly postponed consideration of the proposed tax measure until its next session. When the proposal came up for consideration at that session, it not only died in committee, but the Assembly enacted the famous "Virginia Bill for Religious Liberty" originally written by Thomas Jefferson. The preamble to that Bill stated among other things that

Almighty God hath created the mind free; that all attempts to influence it by temporal punishments or burthens, or by civil incapacitations, tend only to beget habits of hypocrisy and meanness, and are a departure from the plan of the Holy author of our religion, who being Lord both of body and mind, yet chose not to propagate it by coercions on either . . . ; that to compel a man to furnish contributions of money for the propagation of opinions which he disbelieves is sinful and tyrannical; that even the forcing him to support this or that teacher of his own religious persuasion is depriving him of the comfortable liberty of giving his contributions to the particular pastor whose morals he would make his pattern.

And the statute itself enacted

That no man shall be compelled to frequent or support any religious worship, place, or ministry whatsoever,

nor shall be enforced, restrained, molested, or bur-
thened in his body or goods, nor shall otherwise suffer
on account of his religious opinions or belief.

The "establishment of religion" clause of the First
Amendment means at least this: Neither a state nor the
Federal Government can set up a church. Neither can
pass laws which aid one religion, aid all religions, or
prefer one religion over another. Neither can force nor
influence a person to go to or to remain away from
church against his will or force him to profess a belief
or disbelief in any religion. No person can be punished
for entertaining or professing religious beliefs or disbe-
liefs, for church attendance or non-attendance. No tax
in any amount, large or small, can be levied to support
any religious activities or institutions, whatever they
may be called, or whatever form they may adopt to
teach or practice religion. Neither a state nor the Federal Government can, openly or secretly, participate in
the affairs of any religious organizations or groups and
vice versa. In the words of Jefferson, the clause against
establishment of religion by law was intended to erect
"a wall of separation between Church and State."

We must consider the New Jersey statute in accordance with the foregoing limitations imposed by the
First Amendment. But we must not strike that state
statute down if it is within the state's constitutional
power even though it approaches the verge of that
power. New Jersey cannot, consistently with the "establishment of religion" clause of the First Amendment,
contribute tax-raised funds to the support of an institution which teaches the tenets and faith of any church.
On the other hand, other language of the amendment

commands that New Jersey cannot hamper its citizens
in the free exercise of their own religion. Consequently,
it cannot exclude individual Catholics, Lutherans, Mo-
hammedans, Baptists, Jews, Methodists, Non-believers,
Presbyterians, or the members of any other faith, *because of their faith, or lack of it,* from receiving the benefits of public welfare legislation. While we do not
mean to intimate that a state could not provide transportation only to children attending public schools, we
must be careful, in protecting the citizens of New Jersey against state-established churches, to be sure that
we do not inadvertently prohibit New Jersey from extending its general state law benefits to all its citizens
without regard to their religious belief.

Measured by these standards, we cannot say that the
First Amendment prohibits New Jersey from spending
tax-raised funds to pay the bus fares of parochial school
pupils as a part of a general program under which it
pays the fares of pupils attending public and other
schools. It is undoubtedly true that children are helped
to get to church schools. State-paid policemen, detailed
to protect children going to and from church schools
from the very real hazards of traffic, would serve much
the same purpose and accomplish much the same result as state provisions intended to guarantee free
transportation of a kind which the state deems to be
best for the school children's welfare. And parents
might refuse to risk their children to the serious danger
of traffic accidents going to and from parochial schools,
the approaches to which were not protected by policemen. Similarly, parents might be reluctant to permit
their children to attend schools which the state had cut
off from such general government services as ordinary

police and fire protection, connections for sewage disposal, public highways and sidewalks. Of course, cutting off church schools from these services so separate and so indisputably marked off from the religious function would make it far more difficult for the schools to operate. But such is obviously not the purpose of the First Amendment. That Amendment requires the state to be a neutral in its relations with groups of religious believers and nonbelievers; it does not require the state to be their adversary. State power is no more to be used so as to handicap religions than it is to favor them.

ENGEL V. VITALE,
370 U.S. 421 (1962)

The New Hyde Park, New York, school board directed that a prayer written by the state Board of Regents be recited in school each day. Parents of students challenged the recitation because the prayer was contrary to their own religious beliefs. The New York Court of Appeals upheld the recitation as long as students were not compelled to participate. The Supreme Court, in an opinion by Justice Hugo Black, held that the recitation violated the First Amendment's prohibition on "an establishment of religion" by the government.

Opinion of the Court by Justice Black:

The respondent Board of Education of Union Free School District No. 9, New Hyde Park, New York, acting in its official capacity under state law, directed the School District's principal to cause the following prayer to be said aloud by each class in the presence of a teacher at the beginning of each school day: "Almighty God, we acknowledge our dependence upon Thee, and we beg Thy blessings upon us, our parents, our teachers and our Country."

This daily procedure was adopted on the recommendation of the State Board of Regents, a governmental agency created by the State Constitution to which the New York Legislature has granted broad supervisory, executive, and legislative powers over the State's public school system. These state officials composed the prayer which they recommended and published as a part of their "Statement on Moral and Spiritual Training in the Schools," saying: "We believe that this Statement will be subscribed to by all men and women of good will, and we call upon all of them to aid in giving life to our program."

We think that the constitutional prohibition against laws respecting an establishment of religion must at least mean that in this country it is no part of the business of government to compose official prayers for any group of the American people to recite as a part of a religious program carried on by government.

It is a matter of history that this very practice of establishing governmentally composed prayers for religious services was one of the reasons which caused many of our early colonists to leave England and seek religious freedom in America. The Book of Common Prayer, which was created under governmental direction and which was approved by Acts of Parliament in 1548 and 1549, set out in minute detail the accepted form and content of prayer and other religious ceremonies to be used in the established, tax-supported Church of England. The controversies over the Book and what should be its content repeatedly threatened to disrupt the peace of that country as the accepted forms of prayer in the established church changed with the views of the particular ruler that happened to be in control at the time. Powerful groups representing some of the varying religious views of the people struggled among themselves to impress their particular views upon the Government and obtain amendments of the Book more suitable to their respective notions of how religious services should be conducted in order that the official religious establishment would advance their particular religious beliefs. Other groups, lacking the necessary political power to influence the Government on the matter, decided to leave England and its established church and seek freedom in America from England's governmentally ordained and supported religion.

It is an unfortunate fact of history that when some of the very groups which had most strenuously opposed the established Church of England found themselves sufficiently in control of colonial governments in this country to write their own prayers into law, they passed laws making their own religion the official religion of their respective colonies. Indeed, as late as the time of the Revolutionary War, there were established churches in at least eight of the thirteen former colonies and established religions in at least four of the other five. But the successful Revolution against English political domination was shortly followed by intense opposition to the practice of establishing religion by law.

By the time of the adoption of the Constitution, our history shows that there was a widespread awareness among many Americans of the dangers of a union of Church and State. These people knew, some of them from bitter personal experience, that one of the greatest dangers to the freedom of the individual to worship in his own way lay in the Government's placing its official stamp of approval upon one particular kind of prayer or one particular form of religious services. They knew the anguish, hardship and bitter strife that could come when zealous religious groups struggled with one another to obtain the Government's stamp of approval from each King, Queen, or Protector that came to temporary power. The Constitution was intended to avert a part of this danger by leaving the government of this country in the hands of the people, rather than in the hands of any monarch. But this safeguard was not enough. Our Founders were no more willing to let the content of their prayers and their privilege of praying whenever they pleased be influenced by the ballot box than they were to let these vital matters of personal conscience depend upon the succession of monarchs. The First Amendment was added to the Constitution to stand as a guarantee that neither the power nor the prestige of the Federal Government would be used to control, support or influence the kinds of prayer the American people can say—that the people's religions must not be subjected to the pressures of government for change each time a new political administration is elected to office. Under that Amendment's prohibition against governmental establishment of religion, as reinforced by the provisions of the Fourteenth Amendment, government in this country, be it state or federal, is without power to prescribe by law any particular form of prayer which is to be used as an official prayer in carrying on any program of governmentally sponsored religious activity.

There can be no doubt that New York's state prayer program officially establishes the religious beliefs embodied in the Regents' prayer. The respondents' argument to the contrary, which is largely based upon the contention that the Regents' prayer is "nondenominational" and the fact that the program, as modified and approved by state courts, does not require all pupils to recite the prayer, but permits those who wish to do so to remain silent or be excused from the room, ignores the essential nature of the program's constitutional defects. Neither the fact that the prayer may be denominationally neutral nor the fact that its observance on the part of the students is voluntary can serve to free it from the limitations of the Establishment Clause, as it might from the Free Exercise Clause, of the First Amendment, both of which are operative against the States by virtue of the Fourteenth Amendment. Although these two clauses may, in certain instances, overlap, they forbid two quite different kinds of governmental encroachment upon religious freedom. The Establishment Clause, unlike the Free Exercise Clause, does not depend upon any showing of direct governmental compulsion and is violated by the enactment of laws which establish an official religion whether those laws operate directly to coerce nonobserving individuals or not. This is not to say, of course, that laws officially prescribing a particular form of religious worship do not involve coercion of such individuals. When the power, prestige and financial support of government is placed behind a particular religious belief, the indirect coercive pressure upon religious minorities to conform to the prevailing officially approved religion is plain. But the purposes underlying the Establishment Clause go much further than that. Its first and most immediate purpose rested on the belief that a union of government and religion tends to destroy government and to degrade religion. The history of governmentally established religion, both in England and in this country, showed that whenever government had allied itself with one particular form of religion, the inevitable result had been that it had incurred the hatred, disrespect and even contempt of those who held contrary beliefs. That same history showed that many people had lost their respect for any religion that had relied upon the support for government to spread its faith. The Establishment Clause thus stands as an expression of principle on the part of the Founders of our Constitution that religion is too personal, too sacred, too holy, to permit its "unhallowed perversion" by a civil magistrate.

Another purpose of the Establishment Clause rested upon an awareness of the historical fact that governmentally established religions and religious persecutions go hand in hand. The Founders knew that, only a few years after the Book of Common Prayer became the only accepted form of religious services in the established Church of England, an Act of Uniformity was passed to compel all Englishmen to attend those services and to make it a criminal offense to conduct or attend religious gatherings of any other kind— a law which was consistently flouted by dissenting religious groups in England and which contributed to widespread persecutions of people like John Bunyan who persisted in holding "unlawful [religious] meetings . . . to the great disturbance and distraction of the good subjects of this kingdom." And they knew that similar persecutions had received the sanction of law in several of the colonies in this country soon after the establishment of official religions in those colonies. It was in large part to get completely away from this sort of systematic religious persecution that the Founders brought into being our Nation, our Constitution, and our Bill of Rights, with its prohibition against any governmental establishment of religion. The New York laws officially prescribing the Regents' prayer are inconsistent both with the purposes of the Establishment Clause and with the Establishment Clause itself.

It has been argued that to apply the Constitution in such a way as to prohibit state laws respecting an establishment of religious services in public schools is to indicate a hostility toward religion or toward prayer. Nothing, of course, could be more wrong. The history of man is inseparable from the history of religion. And perhaps it is not too much to say that, since the beginning of that history, many people have devoutly believed that "More things are wrought by prayer than this world dreams of." It was doubtless largely due to men who believed this that there grew up a sentiment that caused men to leave the cross-currents of officially established state religions and religious persecution in Europe and come to this country filled with the hope that they could find a place in which they could pray when they pleased to the God of their faith in the language they chose. And there were men of this same faith in the power of prayer who led the fight for adoption of our Constitution and also for our Bill of Rights with the very guarantees of religious freedom that forbid the sort of governmental activity which New York has attempted here. These men knew that the First Amendment, which tried to put an end to governmental control of religion and of prayer, was not written to destroy either. They knew, rather, that it was written to quiet well-justified fears which nearly all of them felt arising out of an awareness that governments of the past had shackled men's tongues to make them speak only the religious thoughts that government wanted them to speak and to pray only to the God that government wanted them to pray to. It is neither sacrilegious nor antireligious to say that each separate government in this country should stay out of the business of writing or sanctioning official prayers and leave that purely religious function to the people themselves and to those the people choose to look to for religious guidance.

It is true that New York's establishment of its Regents' prayer as an officially approved religious doctrine of that State does not amount to a total establishment of one particular religious sect to the exclusion of all others—that, indeed, the governmental endorsement of that prayer seems relatively insignificant when compared to the governmental encroachments upon religion which were commonplace 200 years ago. To those who may subscribe to the view that, because the Regents' official prayer is so brief and general there can be no danger to religious freedom in its governmental establishment, however, it may be appropriate to say in the words of James Madison, the author of the First Amendment:

> [I]t is proper to take alarm at the first experiment on our liberties. . . . Who does not see that the same authority which can establish Christianity, in exclusion of all other Religions, may establish with the same ease

any particular sect of Christians, in exclusion of all other Sects? That the same authority which can force a citizen to contribute three pence only of his property for the support of any one establishment, may force him to conform to any other establishment in all cases whatsoever?

LEE V. WEISMAN, 505 U.S. 577 (1992)

🖙 The principal of a Providence, Rhode Island, middle school asked a rabbi to deliver a prayer at the school's graduation ceremony. Members of the clergy had traditionally been invited to deliver an invocation and benediction and were advised that the prayers should be nonsectarian. Deborah Weisman, a student at the school, challenged the practice, alleging that the prayers violated the Establishment Clause of the First Amendment. The Supreme Court, in an opinion by Justice Anthony Kennedy, agreed, concluding that even nonsectarian prayers at events that were nominally voluntary constituted an establishment of religion. Justice Harry Blackmun concurred, emphasizing that voluntariness or coercion was not the issue; the First Amendment prohibits the government from engaging in religious activities even if participation is voluntary.

Opinion of the Court by Justice Kennedy:

These dominant facts mark and control the confines of our decision: State officials direct the performance of a

formal religious exercise at promotional and graduation ceremonies for secondary schools. Even for those
students who object to the religious exercise, their attendance and participation in the state-sponsored religious activity are, in a fair and real sense, obligatory,
though the school district does not require attendance
as a condition for receipt of the diploma.

The principle that government may accommodate
the free exercise of religion does not supersede the fundamental limitations imposed by the Establishment
Clause. It is beyond dispute that, at a minimum, the
Constitution guarantees that government may not coerce anyone to support or participate in religion or its
exercise, or otherwise act in a way which "establishes a
[state] religion or religious faith, or tends to do so." The
State's involvement in the school prayers challenged
today violates these central principles.

That involvement is as troubling as it is undenied. A
school official, the principal, decided that an invocation
and a benediction should be given; this is a choice attributable to the State, and from a constitutional per-
spective, it is as if a state statute decreed that the prayers
must occur. The principal chose the religious participant, here a rabbi, and that choice is also attributable to
the State.

The First Amendment's Religion Clauses mean that
religious beliefs and religious expression are too precious to be either proscribed or prescribed by the State.
The design of the Constitution is that preservation and
transmission of religious beliefs and worship is a responsibility and a choice committed to the private
sphere, which itself is promised freedom to pursue that
mission. It must not be forgotten, then, that, while con-

cern must be given to define the protection granted to an objector or a dissenting nonbeliever, these same Clauses exist to protect religion from government interference.

The lessons of the First Amendment are as urgent in the modern world as in the 18th Century, when it was written. One timeless lesson is that, if citizens are subjected to state-sponsored religious exercises, the State disavows its own duty to guard and respect that sphere of inviolable conscience and belief which is the mark of a free people. To compromise that principle today would be to deny our own tradition and forfeit our standing to urge others to secure the protections of that tradition for themselves.

As we have observed before, there are heightened concerns with protecting freedom of conscience from subtle coercive pressure in the elementary and secondary public schools.

Law reaches past formalism. And to say a teenage student has a real choice not to attend her high school graduation is formalistic in the extreme. Everyone knows that, in our society and in our culture, high school graduation is one of life's most significant occasions. A school rule which excuses attendance is beside the point. Attendance may not be required by official decree, yet it is apparent that a student is not free to absent herself from the graduation exercise in any real sense of the term "voluntary," for absence would require forfeiture of those intangible benefits which have motivated the student through youth and all her high school years. Graduation is a time for family and those closest to the student to celebrate success and express mutual wishes of gratitude and respect, all to the end of impressing upon the young person the role that it is his or her right and duty to assume in the community and all of its diverse parts.

The importance of the event is the point the school district and the United States rely upon to argue that a formal prayer ought to be permitted, but it becomes one of the principal reasons why their argument must fail. Their contention, one of considerable force were it not for the constitutional constraints applied to state action, is that the prayers are an essential part of these ceremonies because, for many persons, an occasion of this significance lacks meaning if there is no recognition, however brief, that human achievements cannot be understood apart from their spiritual essence. While in some societies the wishes of the majority might prevail, the Establishment Clause of the First Amendment is addressed to this contingency, and rejects the balance urged upon us. The Constitution forbids the State to exact religious conformity from a student as the price of attending her own high school graduation. This is the calculus the Constitution commands.

We do not hold that every state action implicating religion is invalid if one or a few citizens find it offensive. People may take offense at all manner of religious as well as nonreligious messages, but offense alone does not in every case show a violation. We know too that sometimes to endure social isolation or even anger may be the price of conscience or nonconformity. But, by any reading of our cases, the conformity required of the student in this case was too high an exaction to withstand the test of the Establishment Clause. The prayer exercises in this case are especially improper because the State has in every practical sense compelled attendance and participation in an explicit religious exercise at an event of singular importance to every student, one the objecting student had no real alternative to avoid.

Justice Blackmun concurring, joined by Justices Stevens and O'Connor:

I join the Court's opinion today because I find nothing in it inconsistent with the essential precepts of the Establishment Clause developed in our precedents. The Court holds that the graduation prayer is unconstitutional because the State "in effect required participation in a religious exercise." Although our precedents make clear that proof of government coercion is not necessary to prove an Establishment Clause violation, it is sufficient. Government pressure to participate in a religious activity is an obvious indication that the government is endorsing or promoting religion.

But it is not enough that the government restrain from compelling religious practices: it must not engage in them either. The Court repeatedly has recognized that a violation of the Establishment Clause is not predicated on coercion. The Establishment Clause proscribes public schools from "conveying or attempting to convey a message that religion or a particular religious belief is *favored* or *preferred.*"

The mixing of government and religion can be a threat to free government, even if no one is forced to participate. When the government puts its imprimatur on a particular religion, it conveys a message of exclusion to all those who do not adhere to the favored beliefs. A government cannot be premised on the belief that all persons are created equal when it asserts that

God prefers some. Only "anguish, hardship and bitter strife" result "when zealous religious groups struggle with one another to obtain the Government's stamp of approval." Such a struggle can "strain a political system to the breaking point."

When the government arrogates to itself a role in religious affairs, it abandons its obligation as guarantor of democracy. Democracy requires the nourishment of dialogue and dissent, while religious faith puts its trust in an ultimate divine authority above all human deliberation. When the government appropriates religious truth, it "transforms rational debate into theological decree."

CHURCH OF LUKUMI BABALU AYE, INC. V. CITY OF HIALEAH, 508 U.S. 520 (1993)

The Santeria religion is a fusion of the traditional African religion of Yoruba that people brought to Cuba as slaves with elements of Roman Catholicism. Animal sacrifices are offered as part of the religion's practice in rituals for birth, marriage, death, and other events. When the opening of a Santeria church was proposed for Hialeah, Florida, the city council adopted ordinances prohibiting animal sacrifices. The church challenged the ordinances as infringements on the members' free exercise of religion, and the Supreme Court, in an opinion by Justice Anthony Kennedy, agreed.

Opinion of the Court by Justice Kennedy:

In addressing the constitutional protection for free exercise of religion, our cases establish the general proposition that a law that is neutral and of general applicability need not be justified by a compelling governmental interest even if the law has the incidental effect of burdening a particular religious practice. A law failing to satisfy these requirements must be justified by a compelling governmental interest, and must be narrowly tailored to advance that interest.

In our Establishment Clause cases, we have often stated the principle that the First Amendment forbids an official purpose to disapprove of a particular religion or of religion in general. These cases, however, for the most part, have addressed governmental efforts to benefit religion or particular religions, and so have dealt with a question different, at least in its formulation and emphasis, from the issue here. Petitioners allege an attempt to disfavor their religion because of the religious ceremonies it commands, and the Free Exercise Clause is dispositive in our analysis.

At a minimum, the protections of the Free Exercise Clause pertain if the law at issue discriminates against some or all religious beliefs or regulates or prohibits conduct because it is undertaken for religious reasons. Indeed, it was "historical instances of religious persecution and intolerance that gave concern to those who drafted the Free Exercise Clause."

The principle that government, in pursuit of legitimate interests, cannot in a selective manner impose burdens only on conduct motivated by religious belief is essential to the protection of the rights guaranteed by the Free Exercise Clause.

A law burdening religious practice that is not neutral or not of general application must undergo the most rigorous of scrutiny. To satisfy the commands of the First Amendment, a law restrictive of religious practice must advance "interests of the highest order," and must be narrowly tailored in pursuit of those interests. The compelling interest standard that we apply is not "watered down" but "really means what it says." A law that targets religious conduct for distinctive treatment or advances legitimate governmental interests only against conduct with a religious motivation will survive strict scrutiny only in rare cases. It follows from what we have already said that these ordinances cannot withstand this scrutiny.

The Free Exercise Clause commits government itself to religious tolerance, and upon even slight suspicion that proposals for state intervention stem from animosity to religion or distrust of its practices, all officials must pause to remember their own high duty to the Constitution and to the rights it secures. Those in office must be resolute in resisting importunate demands and must ensure that the sole reasons for imposing the burdens of law and regulation are secular. Legislators may not devise mechanisms, overt or disguised, designed to persecute or oppress a religion or its practices. The laws here in question were enacted contrary to these constitutional principles, and they are void.

EMPLOYMENT DIVISION, DEPARTMENT OF HUMAN RESOURCES OF OREGON V. SMITH, 494 U.S. 872 (1990)

☞ Alfred Smith and Galen Black were fired from their jobs at a drug rehab center because they used peyote as part of their worship at a ceremony of the Native American Church. The state employment division denied them unemployment compensation benefits because they had been fired for "misconduct"; the use of peyote, a hallucinogen, is prohibited by state law. They sued, claiming that the state's criminalization of peyote when used for sacramental purposes abridged their right of free exercise of religion. The Supreme Court rejected their claim in an opinion by Justice Antonin Scalia, stating that "neutral, generally applicable" laws did not unconstitutionally burden conduct just because it was religiously motivated. Justice O'Connor concurred in the judgment but offered a different approach, arguing that Justice Scalia applied the wrong constitutional standard: the Oregon law did burden the free exercise of religion, but the state had a compelling interest in doing so, to prevent the harm caused by drug use.

Opinion of the Court by Justice Antonin Scalia:

The Free Exercise Clause of the First Amendment, which has been made applicable to the States by incorporation into the Fourteenth Amendment, provides that "Congress shall make no law respecting an establishment of religion, or *prohibiting the free exercise thereof. . . .*" The free exercise of religion means, first and foremost, the right to believe and profess whatever religious doctrine one desires. Thus, the First Amendment obviously excludes all "governmental regulation of religious *beliefs* as such." The government may not compel affirmation of religious belief, punish the expression of religious doctrines it believes to be false, impose special disabilities on the basis of religious views or religious status, or lend its power to one or the other side in controversies over religious authority or dogma.

But the "exercise of religion" often involves not only belief and profession but the performance of (or abstention from) physical acts: assembling with others for a worship service, participating in sacramental use of bread and wine, proselytizing, abstaining from certain foods or certain modes of transportation. It would be true, we think (though no case of ours has involved the point), that a state would be "prohibiting the free exercise [of religion]" if it sought to ban such acts or abstentions only when they are engaged in for religious reasons, or only because of the religious belief that they display. It would doubtless be unconstitutional, for example, to ban the casting of "statues that are to be used for worship purposes," or to prohibit bowing down before a golden calf.

Respondents in the present case, however, seek to carry the meaning of "prohibiting the free exercise [of religion]" one large step further. They contend that their religious motivation for using peyote places them beyond the reach of a criminal law that is not specifically directed at their religious practice, and that is concededly constitutional as applied to those who use the drug for other reasons. They assert, in other words, that "prohibiting the free exercise [of religion]" includes requiring any individual to observe a generally applicable law that requires (or forbids) the performance of an act that his religious belief forbids (or requires). As a textual matter, we do not think the words must be given that meaning. It is no more necessary to regard the collection of a general tax, for example, as "prohibiting the free exercise [of religion]" by those citizens who believe support of organized government to be sinful than it is to regard the same tax as "abridging the freedom . . . of the press" of those publishing companies that must pay the tax as a condition of staying in business. It is a permissible reading of the text, in the one case as in the other, to say that, if prohibiting the exercise of religion (or burdening the activity of printing) is not the object of the tax, but merely the incidental effect of a generally applicable and otherwise valid provision, the First Amendment has not been offended.

We have never held that an individual's religious beliefs excuse him from compliance with an otherwise valid law prohibiting conduct that the State is free to regulate. On the contrary, the record of more than a century of our free exercise jurisprudence contradicts that proposition. "Laws," we said, "are made for the government of actions, and while they cannot interfere with mere religious belief and opinions, they may with practices. . . . Can a man excuse his practices to the contrary because of his religious belief? To permit this would be to make the professed doctrines of religious belief superior to the law of the land, and in effect to permit every citizen to become a law unto himself."

Subsequent decisions have consistently held that the

right of free exercise does not relieve an individual of the obligation to comply with a "valid and neutral law of general applicability on the ground that the law proscribes (or prescribes) conduct that his religion prescribes (or proscribes)."

Values that are protected against government interference through enshrinement in the Bill of Rights are not thereby banished from the political process. Just as a society that believes in the negative protection accorded to the press by the First Amendment is likely to enact laws that affirmatively foster the dissemination of the printed word, so also a society that believes in the negative protection accorded to religious belief can be expected to be solicitous of that value in its legislation as well. It is therefore not surprising that a number of States have made an exception to their drug laws for sacramental peyote use. But to say that a nondiscriminatory religious practice exemption is permitted, or even that it is desirable, is not to say that it is constitutionally required, and that the appropriate occasions for its creation can be discerned by the courts. It may fairly be said that leaving accommodation to the political process will place at a relative disadvantage those religious practices that are not widely engaged in; but that unavoidable consequence of democratic government must be preferred to a system in which each conscience is a law unto itself or in which judges weigh the social importance of all laws against the centrality of all religious beliefs.

Justice O'Connor, concurring:

Because the First Amendment does not distinguish between religious belief and religious conduct, conduct motivated by sincere religious belief, like the belief itself, must be at least presumptively protected by the Free Exercise Clause.

The Court today, however, interprets the Clause to permit the government to prohibit, without justification, conduct mandated by an individual's religious beliefs, so long as that prohibition is generally applicable. But a law that prohibits certain conduct—conduct that happens to be an act of worship for someone—manifestly does prohibit that person's free exercise of his religion. A person who is barred from engaging in religiously motivated conduct is barred from freely exercising his religion. Moreover, that person is barred from freely exercising his religion regardless of whether the law prohibits the conduct only when engaged in for religious reasons, only by members of that religion, or by all persons. It is difficult to deny that a law that prohibits religiously motivated conduct, even if the law is generally applicable, does not at least implicate First Amendment concerns.

To say that a person's right to free exercise has been burdened, of course, does not mean that he has an absolute right to engage in the conduct. Under our established First Amendment jurisprudence, we have recognized that the freedom to act, unlike the freedom to believe, cannot be absolute. Instead, we have respected both the First Amendment's express textual mandate and the governmental interest in regulation of conduct by requiring the government to justify any substantial burden on religiously motivated conduct by a compelling state interest and by means narrowly tailored to achieve that interest. The compelling interest test effectuates the First Amendment's command that religious liberty is an independent liberty, that it occupies a preferred position, and that the Court will not permit encroachments upon this liberty, whether direct or indirect, unless required by clear and compelling governmental interests "of the highest order." "Only an especially important governmental interest pursued by narrowly tailored means can justify exacting a sacrifice of First Amendment freedoms as the price for an equal share of the rights, benefits, and privileges enjoyed by other citizens."

Chapter 4

CIVIL RIGHTS

SCOTT V. SANDFORD, 60 U.S. 393 (1857)

☞ *Scott v. Sandford* is better known as the *Dred Scott* case. Scott was a slave who sued his owner, claiming that he was free because his former owner had taken him to Illinois, a free state, and the Wisconsin Territory, where Congress had prohibited slavery by the Missouri Compromise of 1820. The Supreme Court, in an opinion by Chief Justice Roger Taney, held that the Missouri Compromise was unconstitutional because it deprived Southerners of their property rights in slaves, and that Scott could not bring the suit anyway because blacks could never be citizens of the United States. The Court's decision outraged Northerners and abolitionists and became an issue in Abraham Lincoln's campaign for the presidency in 1860.

The *Dred Scott* case is an early example of the Court's involvement in race relations, demonstrating an attitude that would be changed by the Civil War, the Reconstruction Amendments, and eventually the civil rights movement and the decisions that movement spawned.

Opinion of the Court by Chief Justice Taney:

The words "people of the United States" and "citizens" are synonymous terms, and mean the same thing. They both describe the political body who, according to our republican institutions, form the sovereignty and who hold the power and conduct the Government through their representatives. They are what we familiarly call the "sovereign people," and every citizen is one of this people, and a constituent member of this sovereignty. The question before us is whether the class of persons described in the plea in abatement compose a portion of this people, and are constituent members of this sovereignty? We think they are not, and that they are not included, and were not intended to be included, under the word "citizens" in the Constitution, and can therefore claim none of the rights and privileges which that instrument provides for and secures to citizens of the United States. On the contrary, they were at that time considered as a subordinate and inferior class of beings who had been subjugated by the dominant race, and, whether emancipated or not, yet remained subject to their authority, and had no rights or privileges but such as those who held the power and the Government might choose to grant them.

It is not the province of the court to decide upon the justice or injustice, the policy or impolicy, of these laws. The decision of that question belonged to the political or lawmaking power, to those who formed the sovereignty and framed the Constitution. The duty of the court is to interpret the instrument they have framed with the best lights we can obtain on the subject, and to administer it as we find it, according to its true intent and meaning when it was adopted.

In the opinion of the court, the legislation and histories of the times, and the language used in the Declaration of Independence, show that neither the class of persons who had been imported as slaves nor their descendants, whether they had become free or not, were then acknowledged as a part of the people, nor intended to be included in the general words used in that memorable instrument.

They had for more than a century before been regarded as beings of an inferior order, and altogether unfit to associate with the white race either in social or political relations, and so far inferior that they had no rights which the white man was bound to respect, and that the negro might justly and lawfully be reduced to slavery for his benefit. He was bought and sold, and treated as an ordinary article of merchandise and traffic whenever a profit could be made by it. This opinion was at that time fixed and universal in the civilized portion of the white race. It was regarded as an axiom in morals as well as in politics which no one thought of disputing or supposed to be open to dispute, and men in every grade and position in society daily and habitually acted upon it in their private pursuits, as well as in matters of public concern, without doubting for a moment the correctness of this opinion.

And in no nation was this opinion more firmly fixed or more uniformly acted upon than by the English Government and English people. They not only seized them on the coast of Africa and sold them or held them in slavery for their own use, but they took them as ordinary articles of merchandise to every country where they could make a profit on them, and were far more extensively engaged in this commerce than any other nation in the world.

The opinion thus entertained and acted upon in England was naturally impressed upon the colonies they founded on this side of the Atlantic. And, accordingly, a negro of the African race was regarded by them as an article of property, and held, and bought and sold as such, in every one of the thirteen colonies which united in the Declaration of Independence and afterwards formed the Constitution of the United States. The slaves were more or less numerous in the different colonies as slave labor was found more or less profitable. But no one seems to have doubted the correctness of the prevailing opinion of the time.

PLESSY V. FERGUSON, 163 U.S. 537 (1896)

The Civil War and the enactment of the Thirteenth, Fourteenth, and Fifteenth Amendments ended slavery but did not remedy racial injustice in America. Following the end of Reconstruction, Southern states adopted new, stringent Jim Crow laws to enforce segregation. One of these was a Louisiana law that required "equal but separate accommodations" for "white" and "colored" railroad passengers. Homer Plessy, who alleged that he was seven-eighths Caucasian and one-eighth of African descent, sued when he was removed from the whites-only section of a first-class railroad car. In an opinion by Justice Henry Brown, the Supreme Court upheld "separate but equal." Justice John Marshall Harlan, a former slave owner, famously dissented, arguing that "separate but equal" was a means of domination by the white race and accurately predicting that *Plessy* would someday be as infamous a decision as *Dred Scott*.

Opinion of the Court by Justice Brown:

By the Fourteenth Amendment, all persons born or naturalized in the United States and subject to the jurisdiction thereof are made citizens of the United States and of the State wherein they reside, and the States are forbidden from making or enforcing any law which shall abridge the privileges or immunities of citizens of the United States, or shall deprive any person of life, liberty, or property without due process of law, or deny to any person within their jurisdiction the equal protection of the laws.

The object of the amendment was undoubtedly to enforce the absolute equality of the two races before the law, but, in the nature of things, it could not have been intended to abolish distinctions based upon color, or to enforce social, as distinguished from political, equality, or a commingling of the two races upon terms unsatisfactory to either. Laws permitting, and even requiring, their separation in places where they are liable to be brought into contact do not necessarily imply the inferiority of either race to the other, and have been generally, if not universally, recognized as within the competency of the state legislatures in the exercise of their police power. The most common instance of this is connected with the establishment of separate schools for white and colored children, which has been held to be a valid exercise of the legislative power even by courts of States where the political rights of the colored race have been longest and most earnestly enforced.

It is claimed by the plaintiff in error that, in any mixed community, the reputation of belonging to the dominant race, in this instance the white race, is property in the same sense that a right of action or of inheritance is property. Conceding this to be so for the purposes of this case, we are unable to see how this statute deprives him of, or in any way affects his right to, such property. If he be a white man and assigned to a colored coach, he may have his action for damages against the company for being deprived of his so-called property. Upon the other hand, if he be a colored man and be so assigned, he has been deprived of no property, since he is not lawfully entitled to the reputation of being a white man.

We consider the underlying fallacy of the plaintiff's argument to consist in the assumption that the enforced separation of the two races stamps the colored race with a badge of inferiority. If this be so, it is not by reason of anything found in the act, but solely because the colored race chooses to put that construction upon it. The argument necessarily assumes that if, as has been more than once the case and is not unlikely to be so again, the colored race should become the dominant power in the state legislature, and should enact a law in precisely similar terms, it would thereby relegate the white race to an inferior position. We imagine that the white race, at least, would not acquiesce in this assumption. The argument also assumes that social prejudices may be overcome by legislation, and that equal rights cannot be secured to the negro except by an enforced commingling of the two races. We cannot accept this proposition. If the two races are to meet upon terms of social equality, it must be the result of natural affinities, a mutual appreciation of each other's merits, and a voluntary consent of individuals. As was said by the Court of Appeals of New York in *People v. Gallagher,* 93 N.Y. 438 (1883),

> this end can neither be accomplished nor promoted by laws which conflict with the general sentiment of the community upon whom they are designed to operate. When the government, therefore, has secured to each of its citizens equal rights before the law and equal opportunities for improvement and progress, it has accomplished the end for which it was organized, and performed all of the functions respecting social advantages with which it is endowed.

Legislation is powerless to eradicate racial instincts or to abolish distinctions based upon physical differences, and the attempt to do so can only result in accentuating the difficulties of the present situation. If the civil and political rights of both races be equal, one cannot be inferior to the other civilly or politically. If one race be inferior to the other socially, the Constitution of the United States cannot put them upon the same plane.

Justice Harlan, dissenting:

In respect of civil rights common to all citizens, the Constitution of the United States does not, I think, permit any public authority to know the race of those entitled to be protected in the enjoyment of such rights.

Every true man has pride of race, and, under appropriate circumstances, when the rights of others, his equals before the law, are not to be affected, it is his privilege to express such pride and to take such action based upon it as to him seems proper. But I deny that any legislative body or judicial tribunal may have regard to the race of citizens when the civil rights of those citizens are involved. Indeed, such legislation as that here in question is inconsistent not only with that equality of rights which pertains to citizenship, National and State, but with the personal liberty enjoyed by everyone within the United States.

It was said in argument that the statute of Louisiana does not discriminate against either race, but prescribes a rule applicable alike to white and colored citizens. But this argument does not meet the difficulty. Everyone knows that the statute in question had its origin in the purpose not so much to exclude white persons from railroad cars occupied by blacks as to exclude colored people from coaches occupied by or assigned to white persons. Railroad corporations of Louisiana did not make discrimination among whites in the matter of accommodation for travelers. The thing to accomplish was, under the guise of giving equal accommodation for whites and blacks, to compel the latter to keep to themselves while traveling in railroad passenger coaches. No one would be so wanting in candor as to assert the contrary. The fundamental objection, therefore, to the statute is that it interferes with the personal freedom of citizens. "Personal liberty," it has been well said, "consists in the power of locomotion, of changing situation, or removing one's person to whatsoever places one's own inclination may direct, without imprisonment or restraint unless by due course of law." If a white man and a black man choose to occupy the same public conveyance on a public highway, it is their right to do so, and no government, proceeding alone on grounds of race, can prevent it without infringing the personal liberty of each.

In my opinion, the judgment this day rendered will, in time, prove to be quite as pernicious as the decision made by this tribunal in the *Dred Scott Case.* It was adjudged in that case that the descendants of Africans who were imported into this country and sold as slaves were not included nor intended to be included under the word "citizens" in the Constitution, and could not claim any of the rights and privileges which that instrument provided for and secured to citizens of the United States; that, at the time of the adoption of the Constitution, they were "considered as a subordinate and inferior class of beings, who had been subjugated by the dominant race, and, whether emancipated or not, yet remained subject to their authority, and had no rights or privileges but such as those who held the power and the government might choose to grant them." The recent amendments of the Constitution, it was supposed, had eradicated these principles from our institutions. But it seems that we have yet, in some of the States, a dominant race—a superior class of citizens, which assumes to regulate the enjoyment of civil rights, common to all citizens, upon the basis of race. The present decision, it may well be apprehended, will not only stimulate aggressions, more or less brutal and irritating, upon the admitted rights of colored citizens, but will encourage the belief that it is possible, by means of state enactments, to defeat the beneficent purposes which the people of the United States had in view when they adopted the recent amendments of the Constitution, by one of which the blacks of this country were made citizens of the United States and of the States in which they respectively reside, and whose privileges and immunities, as citizens, the States are forbidden to abridge. Sixty millions of whites are in no danger from the presence here of eight millions of blacks. The destinies of the two races in this country are indissolubly linked together, and the interests of both require that the common government of all shall not permit the seeds of race hate to be planted under the sanction of law. What can more certainly arouse race hate, what more certainly create and perpetuate a feeling of distrust between these races, than state enactments which, in fact, proceed on the ground that colored citizens are so inferior and degraded that they cannot be allowed to sit in public coaches occupied by white citizens. That, as all will admit, is the real meaning of such legislation as was enacted in Louisiana.

The sure guarantee of the peace and security of each race is the clear, distinct, unconditional recognition by our governments, National and State, of every right that inheres in civil freedom, and of the equality before the law of all citizens of the United States, without regard to race. State enactments regulating the enjoyment of civil rights upon the basis of race, and cunningly devised to defeat legitimate results of the war under the pretence of recognizing equality of rights, can have no other result than to render permanent peace impossible and to keep alive a conflict of races, the continuance of which must do harm to all concerned. This question is not met by the suggestion that social equality cannot exist between the white and black races in this country. That argument, if it can be properly regarded as one, is scarcely worthy of consideration, for social equality no more exists between two races when traveling in a passenger coach or a public highway than when members of the same races sit by each other in a street car or in the jury box, or stand or sit with each other in a political assembly, or when they use in common the street of a city or town, or when they are in the same room for the purpose of having their names placed on the registry of voters, or when they approach the ballot box in order to exercise the high privilege of voting.

The arbitrary separation of citizens on the basis of race while they are on a public highway is a badge of servitude wholly inconsistent with the civil freedom and the equality before the law established by the Constitution. It cannot be justified upon any legal grounds.

If evils will result from the commingling of the two races upon public highways established for the benefit of all, they will be infinitely less than those that will surely come from state legislation regulating the enjoyment of civil rights upon the basis of race. We boast of the freedom enjoyed by our people above all other peoples. But it is difficult to reconcile that boast with a state of the law which, practically, puts the brand of servitude and degradation upon a large class of our fellow citizens, our equals before the law. The thin disguise of "equal" accommodations for passengers in railroad coaches will not mislead anyone, nor atone for the wrong this day done.

BROWN V. BOARD OF EDUCATION OF TOPEKA, 347 U.S. 483 (1954)

✒️ *Brown v. Board of Education* is one of the most famous and important cases the U.S. Supreme Court has
ever decided. The NAACP Legal Defense Fund, led by
Thurgood Marshall, who would later become the first
African American to sit on the Supreme Court, mounted
a decades-long campaign to end segregation. The campaign challenged the absence of equal educational opportunities for blacks, the inequality of supposed
"separate but equal" graduate programs, and finally, in
Brown, the doctrine of "separate but equal" itself. The
Supreme Court, in an opinion by Chief Justice Earl
Warren, held that separate facilities were "inherently
unequal" and therefore unconstitutional; it was subsequently reported that Warren worked heroically behind
the scenes to make sure that the decision was unanimous.

The decision in *Brown* did not immediately end segregation, of course. Resistance in the Southern states
was massive, leading in a few years to the Court's decision in *Cooper v. Aaron* demanding obedience to its decision (discussed in chapter 1), civil rights legislation,
and sit-ins and demonstrations by civil rights activists.
Nevertheless, *Brown* was an important statement of the
values of equality toward which the United States was
evolving.

Opinion of the Court by Chief Justice Warren:

In the first cases in this Court construing the Fourteenth Amendment, decided shortly after its adoption, the Court interpreted it as proscribing all state-imposed discriminations against the Negro race. The doctrine of "separate but equal" did not make its appearance in this Court until 1896 in the case of *Plessy v. Ferguson, supra,* involving not education but transportation. American courts have since labored with the doctrine for over half a century.

Here there are findings below that the Negro and white schools involved have been equalized, or are being equalized, with respect to buildings, curricula, qualifications and salaries of teachers, and other "tangible" factors. Our decision, therefore, cannot turn on merely a comparison of these tangible factors in the Negro and white schools involved in each of the cases. We must look instead to the effect of segregation itself on public education.

In approaching this problem, we cannot turn the clock back to 1868, when the Amendment was adopted, or even to 1896, when *Plessy v. Ferguson* was written. We must consider public education in the light of its full development and its present place in American life throughout the Nation. Only in this way can it be determined if segregation in public schools deprives these plaintiffs of the equal protection of the laws.

Today, education is perhaps the most important function of state and local governments. Compulsory school attendance laws and the great expenditures for education both demonstrate our recognition of the importance of education to our democratic society. It is required in the performance of our most basic public responsibilities, even service in the armed forces. It is the very foundation of good citizenship. Today it is a principal instrument in awakening the child to cultural values, in preparing him for later professional training, and in helping him to adjust normally to his environment. In these days, it is doubtful that any child may reasonably be expected to succeed in life if he is denied the opportunity of an education. Such an opportunity, where the state has undertaken to provide it, is a right which must be made available to all on equal terms.

We come then to the question presented: Does segregation of children in public schools solely on the basis of race, even though the physical facilities and other "tangible" factors may be equal, deprive the children of the minority group of equal educational opportunities? We believe that it does.

To separate them from others of similar age and qualifications solely because of their race generates a feeling of inferiority as to their status in the community that may affect their hearts and minds in a way unlikely ever to be undone. The effect of this separation on their educational opportunities was well stated by a finding in the Kansas case by a court which nevertheless felt compelled to rule against the Negro plaintiffs: "Segregation of white and colored children in public schools has a detrimental effect upon the colored children. The impact is greater when it has the sanction of the law, for the policy of separating the races is usually interpreted as denoting the inferiority of the negro group. A sense of inferiority affects the motivation of a child to learn. Segregation with the sanction of law, therefore, has a tendency to [retard] the educational and mental development of negro children and to deprive them of some of the benefits they would receive in a racial[ly] integrated school system."Whatever may have been the extent of psychological knowledge at the time of *Plessy v. Ferguson*, this finding is amply supported by modern authority. Any language in *Plessy v. Ferguson* contrary to this finding is rejected.

We conclude that, in the field of public education, the doctrine of "separate but equal" has no place. Separate educational facilities are inherently unequal. Therefore, we hold that the plaintiffs and others similarly situated for whom the actions have been brought are, by reason of the segregation complained of, deprived of the equal protection of the laws guaranteed by the Fourteenth Amendment.

GRUTTER V. BOLLINGER, 539 U.S. 306 (2003)

Grutter v. Bollinger and its companion case, *Gratz v. Bollinger*, 539 U.S. 244 (2003), involved affirmative action programs in higher education. In both cases, white applicants alleged that the programs favored minority applicants in an unconstitutional manner. In *Grutter* the Supreme Court, in an opinion by Justice Sandra Day O'Connor, upheld the affirmative action program at the University of Michigan Law School, while in *Gratz* the Court, in an opinion by Chief Justice William Rehnquist, struck down the university's undergraduate admissions program. Justice O'Connor was the swing vote making a majority in each case. The essential difference between the two cases was that the law school's admissions process involved an individualized review of each applicant in which race was a factor, but the undergraduate program used a point system and automatically awarded twenty points of the one hundred needed to gain admission to African American, Native American, and Hispanic applicants.

In *Grutter*, Justice Clarence Thomas, the Court's only black member, concurred in part and dissented in part in an opinion that challenged the majority's constitutional analysis and also reflected on the harm done by affirmative action programs.

Opinion of the Court by Justice O'Connor:

We last addressed the use of race in public higher education over 25 years ago. In the landmark *Bakke* case [*Regents of the University of California v. Bakke*, 438 U.S. 265 (1978)], we reviewed a racial set-aside program that reserved 16 out of 100 seats in a medical school class for members of certain minority groups. The decision produced six separate opinions, none of which commanded a majority of the Court. Justice Powell provided a fifth vote not only for invalidating the set-aside program, but also for reversing the state court's injunction against any use of race whatsoever. The only holding for the Court in *Bakke* was that a "State has a substantial interest that legitimately may be served by a properly devised admissions program involving the competitive consideration of race and ethnic origin."

Since this Court's splintered decision in *Bakke*, Justice Powell's opinion announcing the judgment of the

Court has served as the touchstone for constitutional analysis of race-conscious admissions policies.

Justice Powell began by stating that "the guarantee of equal protection cannot mean one thing when applied to one individual and something else when applied to a person of another color. If both are not accorded the same protection, then it is not equal." In Justice Powell's view, when governmental decisions "touch upon an individual's race or ethnic background, he is entitled to a judicial determination that the burden he is asked to bear on that basis is precisely tailored to serve a compelling governmental interest."

The Equal Protection Clause [of the Fourteenth Amendment] provides that no State shall "deny to any person within its jurisdiction the equal protection of the laws." Because the Fourteenth Amendment "protects *persons,* not *groups,*" all "governmental action based on race—a *group* classification long recognized as in most circumstances irrelevant and therefore prohibited—should be subjected to detailed judicial inquiry to ensure that the *personal* right to equal protection of the laws has not been infringed." We are a "free people whose institutions are founded upon the doctrine of equality." It follows from that principle that "government may treat people differently because of their race only for the most compelling reasons."

We have held that all racial classifications imposed by government "must be analyzed by a reviewing court under strict scrutiny." This means that such classifications are constitutional only if they are narrowly tailored to further compelling governmental interests. "Absent searching judicial inquiry into the justification for such race-based measures," we have no way to determine what "classifications are 'benign' or 'remedial' and what classifications are in fact motivated by illegitimate notions of racial inferiority or simple racial politics." We apply strict scrutiny to all racial classifications to "'smoke out' illegitimate uses of race by assuring that [government] is pursuing a goal important enough to warrant use of a highly suspect tool."

Even in the limited circumstance when drawing racial distinctions is permissible to further a compelling state interest, government is still "constrained in how it may pursue that end: [T]he means chosen to accomplish the [government's] asserted purpose must be specifically and narrowly framed to accomplish that purpose."

To be narrowly tailored, a race-conscious admissions program cannot use a quota system—it cannot "insulate each category of applicants with certain desired qualifications from competition with all other applicants." Instead, a university may consider race or ethnicity only as a "'plus' in a particular applicant's file," without "insulating the individual from comparison with all other candidates for the available seats." In other words, an admissions program must be "flexible enough to consider all pertinent elements of diversity in light of the particular qualifications of each applicant, and to place them on the same footing for consideration, although not necessarily according them the same weight."

We acknowledge that "there are serious problems of justice connected with the idea of preference itself." Narrow tailoring, therefore, requires that a race-conscious admissions program not unduly harm members of any racial group. Even remedial race-based governmental action generally "remains subject to continuing oversight to assure that it will work the least harm possible to other innocent persons competing for the benefit." To be narrowly tailored, a race-conscious admissions program must not "unduly burden individuals who are not members of the favored racial and ethnic groups."

We are mindful, however, that "a core purpose of the Fourteenth Amendment was to do away with all governmentally imposed discrimination based on race." Accordingly, race-conscious admissions policies must be limited in time. This requirement reflects that racial classifications, however compelling their goals, are potentially so dangerous that they may be employed no more broadly than the interest demands. Enshrining a permanent justification for racial preferences would offend this fundamental equal protection principle.

Justice Thomas, concurring in part and dissenting in part:

Frederick Douglass, speaking to a group of abolitionists almost 140 years ago, delivered a message lost on today's majority:

> In regard to the colored people, there is always more that is benevolent, I perceive, than just, manifested towards us. What I ask for the negro is not benevolence, not pity, not sympathy, but simply *justice*. The American people have always been anxious to know what they shall do with us. I have had but one answer from the beginning. Do nothing with us! Your doing with us has already played the mischief with us. Do nothing

with us! If the apples will not remain on the tree of
their own strength, if they are worm-eaten at the core,
if they are early ripe and disposed to fall, let them fall!
And if the negro cannot stand on his own legs, let him
fall also. All I ask is, give him a chance to stand on his
own legs! Let him alone! Your interference is doing
him positive injury.

Like Douglass, I believe blacks can achieve in every
avenue of American life without the meddling of university administrators. Because I wish to see all students succeed whatever their color, I share, in some
respect, the sympathies of those who sponsor the type
of discrimination advanced by the University of Michigan Law School. The Constitution does not, however,
tolerate institutional devotion to the status quo in admissions policies when such devotion ripens into racial
discrimination. Nor does the Constitution counte-
nance the unprecedented deference the Court gives to
the Law School, an approach inconsistent with the
very concept of "strict scrutiny."

The Constitution abhors classifications based on
race, not only because those classifications can harm
favored races or are based on illegitimate motives, but
also because every time the government places citizens
on racial registers and makes race relevant to the provision of burdens or benefits, it demeans us all. "Purchased at the price of immeasurable human suffering,
the equal protection principle reflects our Nation's understanding that such classifications ultimately have a
destructive impact on the individual and our society."

It is uncontested that each year, the Law School ad-
mits a handful of blacks who would be admitted in the

absence of racial discrimination. Who can differentiate between those who belong and those who do not? The majority of blacks are admitted to the Law School because of discrimination, and because of this policy all are tarred as undeserving. This problem of stigma does not depend on determinacy as to whether those stigmatized are actually the "beneficiaries" of racial discrimination. When blacks take positions in the highest places of government, industry, or academia, it is an open question today whether their skin color played a part in their advancement. The question itself is the stigma—because either racial discrimination did play a role, in which case the person may be deemed "otherwise unqualified," or it did not, in which case asking the question itself unfairly marks those blacks who would succeed without discrimination. Is this what the Court means by "visibly open"?

Chapter 5

THE RIGHT OF
PRIVACY

MEYER V. NEBRASKA,
262 U.S. 390 (1923)

☞ Robert Meyer taught Bible stories in German at a
Lutheran parochial school in Nebraska, in violation of a
state law that prohibited instruction in a foreign language to students below the ninth grade. He was prosecuted and convicted under the law. The Supreme Court,
in an opinion by Justice James McReynolds, reversed
the conviction, relying on a series of cases interpreting
the Due Process Clauses of the Fifth and Fourteenth
Amendments. These "substantive due process" cases
focused on the content of rights people possessed, as
distinguished from the more familiar "procedural due
process," which specifies procedures the government
must follow when limiting rights.

Opinion of the Court by Justice McReynolds:

The problem for our determination is whether the statute, as construed and applied, unreasonably infringes
the liberty guaranteed to the plaintiff in error by the

Fourteenth Amendment. "No State shall . . . deprive any person of life, liberty, or property, without due process of law."

While this Court has not attempted to define with exactness the liberty thus guaranteed, the term has received much consideration and some of the included things have been definitely stated. Without doubt, it denotes not merely freedom from bodily restraint, but also the right of the individual to contract, to engage in any of the common occupations of life, to acquire useful knowledge, to marry, establish a home and bring up children, to worship God according to the dictates of his own conscience, and generally to enjoy those privileges long recognized at common law as essential to the orderly pursuit of happiness by free men. The established doctrine is that this liberty may not be interfered with, under the guise of protecting the public interest, by legislative action which is arbitrary or without reasonable relation to some purpose within the competency of the state to effect. Determination by the legislature of what constitutes proper exercise of police power is not final or conclusive, but is subject to supervision by the courts.

The American people have always regarded education and acquisition of knowledge as matters of supreme importance which should be diligently promoted. The Ordinance of 1787 declares, "Religion, morality, and knowledge being necessary to good government and the happiness of mankind, schools and the means of education shall forever be encouraged."

Corresponding to the right of control, it is the natural duty of the parent to give his children education suitable to their station in life, and nearly all the states, including Nebraska, enforce this obligation by compulsory laws.

Practically, education of the young is only possible in schools conducted by especially qualified persons who devote themselves thereto. The calling always has been regarded as useful and honorable, essential, indeed, to the public welfare. Mere knowledge of the German language cannot reasonably be regarded as harmful. Heretofore it has been commonly looked upon as helpful and desirable. Plaintiff in error taught this language in school as part of his occupation. His right thus to teach and the right of parents to engage him so to instruct their children, we think, are within the liberty of the amendment.

That the state may do much, go very far, indeed, in order to improve the quality of its citizens, physically, mentally and morally, is clear; but the individual has certain fundamental rights which must be respected. The protection of the Constitution extends to all, to those who speak other languages as well as to those born with English on the tongue. Perhaps it would be highly advantageous if all had ready understanding of our ordinary speech, but this cannot be coerced by methods which conflict with the Constitution—a desirable end cannot be promoted by prohibited means.

The power of the state to compel attendance at some school and to make reasonable regulations for all schools, including a requirement that they shall give instructions in English, is not questioned. Nor has challenge been made of the state's power to prescribe a curriculum for institutions which it supports. . . . No emergency has arisen which renders knowledge by a child of some language other than English so clearly harmful as to justify its inhibition with the consequent infringement of rights long freely enjoyed. We are constrained to conclude that the statute as applied is arbitrary and without reasonable relation to any end within the competency of the state.

GRISWOLD V. CONNECTICUT, 381 U.S. 479 (1965)

☞ Estelle Griswold and Dr. C. Lee Buxton, the executive director and medical director of the Planned Parenthood League of Connecticut, were prosecuted and convicted under a state statute that made it criminal to use contraception or to assist or counsel anyone to do so. They challenged the constitutionality of the statute under the Fourteenth Amendment. The Supreme Court, in an opinion by Justice William O. Douglas, overturned their convictions. In doing so, the Court built on precedents such as *Meyer v. Nebraska*, excerpted in this chapter, and on many parts of the Bill of Rights to develop a broader right of privacy.

Opinion of the Court by Justice Douglas:

We are met with a wide range of questions that implicate the Due Process Clause of the Fourteenth Amendment. We do not sit as a super-legislature to determine the wisdom, need, and propriety of laws that touch economic problems, business affairs, or social conditions. This law, however, operates directly on an intimate relation of husband and wife and their physician's role in one aspect of that relation.

The association of people is not mentioned in the Constitution nor in the Bill of Rights. The right to educate a child in a school of the parents' choice— whether public or private or parochial—is also not mentioned. Nor is the right to study any particular subject or any foreign language. Yet the First Amendment has been construed to include certain of those rights.

By *Pierce v. Society of Sisters*, 268 U.S. 510 (1925), the right to educate one's children as one chooses is made applicable to the States by the force of the First and Fourteenth Amendments. By *Meyer v. State of Nebraska*, 262 U.S. 390 (1923), the same dignity is given the right to study the German language in a private school. In other words, the State may not, consistently with the spirit of the First Amendment, contract the spectrum of available knowledge. The right of freedom of speech and press includes not only the right to utter or to print, but the right to distribute, the right to receive, the right to read and freedom of inquiry, freedom of thought, and freedom to teach; indeed, the freedom of the entire university community. Without those peripheral rights the specific rights would be less secure.

The foregoing cases suggest that specific guarantees in the Bill of Rights have penumbras, formed by emanations from those guarantees that help give them life and substance. Various guarantees create zones of privacy. The right of association contained in the penumbra of the First Amendment is one, as we have seen. The Third Amendment, in its prohibition against the quartering of soldiers "in any house" in time of peace without the consent of the owner, is another facet of that privacy. The Fourth Amendment explicitly affirms the "right of the people to be secure in their persons, houses, papers, and effects, against unreasonable searches and seizures." The Fifth Amendment, in its Self-Incrimination Clause, enables the citizen to create a zone of privacy which government may not force him to surrender to his detriment. The Ninth Amendment provides: "The enumeration in the Constitution, of certain rights, shall not be construed to deny or disparage others retained by the people."

The Fourth and Fifth Amendments were described in *Boyd v. United States*, 116 U.S. 616 (1886), as protection against all governmental invasions "of the sanctity of a man's home and the privacies of life." We recently referred in *Mapp v. Ohio*, 367 U.S. 643 (1961), to the Fourth Amendment as creating a "right to privacy, no less important than any other right carefully and particularly reserved to the people."

We have had many controversies over these penumbral rights of "privacy and repose." These cases bear witness that the right of privacy which presses for recognition here is a legitimate one.

The present case, then, concerns a relationship lying within the zone of privacy created by several fundamental constitutional guarantees. And it concerns a law which, in forbidding the use of contraceptives, rather than regulating their manufacture or sale, seeks to achieve its goals by means having a maximum destructive impact upon that relationship. Such a law cannot stand in light of the familiar principle, so often applied by this Court, that a "governmental purpose to control or prevent activities constitutionally subject to state regulation may not be achieved by means which sweep unnecessarily broadly and thereby invade the area of protected freedoms." Would we allow the police to search the sacred precincts of marital bedrooms for telltale signs of the use of contraceptives? The very idea is repulsive to the notions of privacy surrounding the marriage relationship.

We deal with a right of privacy older than the Bill of Rights—older than our political parties, older than our school system. Marriage is a coming together for better or for worse, hopefully enduring, and intimate to the degree of being sacred. It is an association that promotes a way of life, not causes; a harmony in living, not political faiths; a bilateral loyalty, not commercial or social projects. Yet it is an association for as noble a purpose as any involved in our prior decisions.

PLANNED PARENTHOOD OF SOUTHEASTERN PENNSYLVANIA V. CASEY, 505 U.S. 833 (1992)

The right of privacy received its most controversial application in *Roe v. Wade,* 410 U.S. 113 (1973). In that case the Supreme Court, in an opinion by Justice Harry Blackmun, recognized that previous cases had held that the right of privacy "has some extension to activities relating to marriage, procreation, contraception, family relationships, and child rearing and education." In *Roe* the Court held that the right "is broad enough to encompass a woman's decision whether or not to terminate her pregnancy." During approximately the first trimester of pregnancy, the decision to terminate is left to the pregnant woman and her physician; in the second trimester, the government may regulate the abortion procedure in ways relating to the mother's health; in the third trimester, the government may regulate and even prohibit abortion except where it is necessary for the life or health of the mother.

As the states responded to *Roe v. Wade* with legislation attempting to restrict abortions, the Court decided a number of cases further defining the impact of *Roe* and the right of privacy in this area. In *Planned Parenthood v. Casey*, a divided Court upheld *Roe*'s central holding and adopted a test articulated by Justice Sandra Day O'Connor that focused on whether the state law placed an "undue burden" on a woman's right to choose.

Opinion of the Court by Justice O'Connor:

Liberty finds no refuge in a jurisprudence of doubt. Yet, nineteen years after our holding that the Constitution protects a woman's right to terminate her pregnancy in its early stages, that definition of liberty is still questioned.

It must be stated at the outset and with clarity that *Roe*'s essential holding, the holding we reaffirm, has three parts. First is a recognition of the right of the woman to choose to have an abortion before viability and to obtain it without undue interference from the State. Before viability, the State's interests are not strong enough to support a prohibition of abortion or the imposition of a substantial obstacle to the woman's effective right to elect the procedure. Second is a confirmation of the State's power to restrict abortions after fetal viability if the law contains exceptions for pregnancies which endanger a woman's life or health. And third is the principle that the State has legitimate interests from the outset of the pregnancy in protecting the health of the woman and the life of the fetus that may become a child. These principles do not contradict one another; and we adhere to each.

Constitutional protection of the woman's decision to terminate her pregnancy derives from the Due Process Clause of the Fourteenth Amendment. It declares that no State shall "deprive any person of life, liberty, or property, without due process of law." The controlling word in the case before us is "liberty." Although a literal reading of the Clause might suggest that it governs only the procedures by which a State may deprive persons of liberty, for at least 105 years, the Clause has been understood to contain a substantive component as well, one "barring certain government actions regardless of the fairness of the procedures used to implement them." As Justice Brandeis (joined by Justice Holmes) observed, "Despite arguments to the contrary which had seemed to me persuasive, it is settled that the due process clause of the Fourteenth Amendment applies to matters of substantive law as well as to matters of procedure. Thus all fundamental rights comprised within the term liberty are protected by the Federal Constitution from invasion by the States." "The guaranties of due process, though having their roots in Magna Carta's [guarantee that no one could be punished except through the law of the land] and considered as procedural safeguards 'against executive usurpation and tyranny,' have in this country 'become bulwarks also against arbitrary legislation.'"

The most familiar of the substantive liberties protected by the Fourteenth Amendment are those recognized by the Bill of Rights. We have held that the Due Process Clause of the Fourteenth Amendment incorporates most of the Bill of Rights against the States. It is tempting, as a means of curbing the discretion of federal judges, to suppose that liberty encompasses no more than those rights already guaranteed to the individual against federal interference by the express provisions of the first eight amendments to the Constitution. But of course this Court has never accepted that view.

It is also tempting, for the same reason, to suppose that the Due Process Clause protects only those practices, defined at the most specific level, that were protected against government interference by other rules of law when the Fourteenth Amendment was ratified. But such a view would be inconsistent with our law. It is a promise of the Constitution that there is a realm of personal liberty which the government may not enter. We have vindicated this principle before. Marriage is mentioned nowhere in the Bill of Rights, and interracial marriage was illegal in most States in the 19th century, but the Court was no doubt correct in finding it to be an aspect of liberty protected against state interference by the substantive component of the Due Process Clause.

Neither the Bill of Rights nor the specific practices of States at the time of the adoption of the Fourteenth Amendment marks the outer limits of the substantive sphere of liberty which the Fourteenth Amendment protects. As the second Justice Harlan recognized:

> The full scope of the liberty guaranteed by the Due Process Clause cannot be found in or limited by the precise terms of the specific guarantees elsewhere pro-

vided in the Constitution. This "liberty" is not a series of isolated points pricked out in terms of the taking of property; the freedom of speech, press, and religion; the right to keep and bear arms; the freedom from unreasonable searches and seizures; and so on. It is a rational continuum which, broadly speaking, includes a freedom from all substantial arbitrary impositions and purposeless restraints, and which also recognizes, what a reasonable and sensitive judgment must, that certain interests require particularly careful scrutiny of the state needs asserted to justify their abridgment.

The inescapable fact is that adjudication of substantive due process claims may call upon the Court in interpreting the Constitution to exercise that same capacity which, by tradition, courts always have exercised: reasoned judgment. Its boundaries are not susceptible of expression as a simple rule. That does not mean we are free to invalidate state policy choices with which we disagree; yet neither does it permit us to shrink from the duties of our office. As Justice Harlan observed:

> Due process has not been reduced to any formula; its content cannot be determined by reference to any code. The best that can be said is that, through the course of this Court's decisions, it has represented the balance which our Nation, built upon postulates of respect for the liberty of the individual, has struck between that liberty and the demands of organized society. If the supplying of content to this Constitutional concept has, of necessity, been a rational process, it certainly has not been one where judges have felt free to roam where unguided speculation might take them.

The balance of which I speak is the balance struck by
this country, having regard to what history teaches are
the traditions from which it developed as well as the
traditions from which it broke. That tradition is a living thing. A decision of this Court which radically
departs from it could not long survive, while a decision
which builds on what has survived is likely to be
sound. No formula could serve as a substitute, in this
area, for judgment and restraint."

Men and women of good conscience can disagree,
and we suppose some always shall disagree, about the
profound moral and spiritual implications of terminat-
ing a pregnancy, even in its earliest stage. Some of us as
individuals find abortion offensive to our most basic
principles of morality, but that cannot control our decision. Our obligation is to define the liberty of all, not
to mandate our own moral code.

LAWRENCE V. TEXAS, 539 U.S. 558 (2003)

In *Bowers v. Hardwick,* 478 U.S. 186 (1986), the
Court upheld a Georgia statute criminalizing oral or
anal sex as applied to homosexuals. In an opinion by
Justice Byron White, the Court determined that the
question was whether the fundamental right to privacy
encompassed these acts, and concluded that it did not
because the acts did not involve child rearing, procreation, contraception, or abortion, as earlier cases had.

A decade and a half later, the Court confronted the
same issue again. When Houston police officers arrived
at an apartment in response to a reported weapons dis-

turbance, they saw John Geddes Lawrence and Tyron Garner engaging in a sexual act. Lawrence and Garner were prosecuted under a Texas criminal law punishing "deviant sexual intercourse" and were each fined $200. On appeal, the Supreme Court overruled *Bowers* in an opinion by Justice Anthony Kennedy and held that the right of privacy encompassed private, consensual sex between adults. Justice Antonin Scalia dissented, arguing that because the right to engage in homosexual conduct was not fundamental, it could be regulated by the state.

Opinion of the Court by Justice Kennedy:

Liberty protects the person from unwarranted government intrusions into a dwelling or other private places. In our tradition the State is not omnipresent in the home. And there are other spheres of our lives and existence, outside the home, where the State should not be a dominant presence. Freedom extends beyond spatial bounds. Liberty presumes an autonomy of self that includes freedom of thought, belief, expression, and certain intimate conduct. The instant case involves liberty of the person both in its spatial and more transcendent dimensions.

The Court began its substantive discussion in *Bowers* as follows: "The issue presented is whether the Federal Constitution confers a fundamental right upon homosexuals to engage in sodomy and hence invalidates the laws of the many States that still make such conduct illegal and have done so for a very long time." That statement, we now conclude, discloses the Court's own failure to appreciate the extent of the liberty at stake. To say that the issue in *Bowers* was simply the right to engage in certain sexual conduct demeans the claim the individual put forward, just as it would demean a married couple were it to be said marriage is simply about the right to have sexual intercourse. The laws involved in *Bowers* and here are, to be sure, statutes that purport to do no more than prohibit a particular sexual act. Their penalties and purposes, though, have more far-reaching consequences, touching upon the most private human conduct, sexual behavior, and in the most private of places, the home. The statutes do seek to control a personal relationship that, whether or not entitled to formal recognition in the law, is within the liberty of persons to choose without being punished as criminals.

This, as a general rule, should counsel against attempts by the State, or a court, to define the meaning of the relationship or to set its boundaries absent injury to a person or abuse of an institution the law protects. It suffices for us to acknowledge that adults may choose to enter upon this relationship in the confines of their homes and their own private lives and still retain their dignity as free persons. When sexuality finds overt expression in intimate conduct with another person, the conduct can be but one element in a personal bond that is more enduring. The liberty protected by the Constitution allows homosexual persons the right to make this choice.

The present case does not involve minors. It does not involve persons who might be injured or coerced or who are situated in relationships where consent might not easily be refused. It does not involve public conduct or prostitution. It does not involve whether the government must give formal recognition to any relationship that homosexual persons seek to enter. The case does involve two adults who, with full and mutual consent from each other, engaged in sexual practices common to a homosexual lifestyle. The petitioners are entitled to respect for their private lives. The State cannot demean their existence or control their destiny by making their private sexual conduct a crime. Their right to liberty under the Due Process Clause gives them the full right to engage in their conduct without intervention of the government. "It is a promise of the Constitution that there is a realm of personal liberty which the government may not enter." The Texas statute furthers no legitimate state interest which can justify its intrusion into the personal and private life of the individual.

Had those who drew and ratified the Due Process Clauses of the Fifth Amendment or the Fourteenth Amendment known the components of liberty in its manifold possibilities, they might have been more specific. They did not presume to have this insight. They knew times can blind us to certain truths and later generations can see that laws once thought necessary and proper in fact serve only to oppress. As the Constitution endures, persons in every generation can invoke its principles in their own search for greater freedom.

Justice Scalia, joined by Chief Justice Rehnquist and Justice Thomas, dissenting:

Our opinions applying the doctrine known as "substantive due process" hold that the Due Process Clause prohibits States from infringing *fundamental* liberty interests, unless the infringement is narrowly tailored to serve a compelling state interest. We have held repeatedly, in cases the Court today does not overrule, that *only* fundamental rights qualify for this so-called "heightened scrutiny" protection—that is, rights which are "deeply rooted in this Nation's history and tradition." All other liberty interests may be abridged or abrogated pursuant to a validly enacted state law if that law is rationally related to a legitimate state interest.

Realizing that fact, the Court instead says: "We think that our laws and traditions in the past half century are of most relevance here. These references show *an emerging awareness* that liberty gives substantial protection to adult persons in deciding how to conduct their private lives *in matters pertaining to sex*."

An "emerging awareness" is by definition not "deeply rooted in this Nation's history and traditions," as we have said "fundamental right" status requires. Constitutional entitlements do not spring into existence because some States choose to lessen or eliminate criminal sanctions on certain behavior. Much less do they spring into existence, as the Court seems to believe, because *foreign nations* decriminalize conduct.

One of the most revealing statements in today's opinion is the Court's grim warning that the criminalization of homosexual conduct is "an invitation to subject homosexual persons to discrimination both in the public and in the private spheres." It is clear from this that the Court has taken sides in the culture war, departing from its role of assuring, as neutral observer, that the democratic rules of engagement are observed. Many Americans do not want persons who openly engage in homosexual conduct as partners in their business, as scoutmasters for their children, as teachers in their children's schools, or as boarders in their home. They view this as protecting themselves and their families from a lifestyle that they believe to be immoral and destructive. The Court views it as "discrimination" which it is the function of our judgments to deter. So imbued is the Court with the law profession's anti-anti-homosexual culture, that it is seemingly unaware that the attitudes of that culture are not obviously "mainstream"; that in most States what the Court calls "discrimination" against those who engage in homosexual acts is perfectly legal; that proposals to ban such "discrimination" under Title VII have repeatedly been rejected by Congress; that in some cases such "discrimination" is *mandated* by federal statute; and that in some cases such "discrimination" is a constitutional right, see *Boy Scouts of America v. Dale*, 530 U.S. 640 (2000) [discussed in chapter 2].

Let me be clear that I have nothing against homosexuals, or any other group, promoting their agenda through normal democratic means. Social perceptions of sexual and other morality change over time, and every group has the right to persuade its fellow citizens that its view of such matters is the best. That homosexuals have achieved some success in that enterprise is attested to by the fact that Texas is one of the few remaining States that criminalize private, consensual homosexual acts. But persuading one's fellow citizens is one thing, and imposing one's views in absence of democratic majority will is something else. I would no more *require* a State to criminalize homosexual acts—or, for that matter, display *any* moral disapprobation of them—than I would *forbid* it to do so. What Texas has chosen to do is well within the range of traditional democratic action, and its hand should not be stayed through the invention of a brand-new "constitutional right" by a Court that is impatient of democratic change. It is indeed true that "later generations can see that laws once thought necessary and proper in fact serve only to oppress"; and when that happens, later generations can repeal those laws. But it is the premise of our system that those judgments are to be made by the people, and not imposed by a governing caste that knows best.

One of the benefits of leaving regulation of this matter to the people rather than to the courts is that the people, unlike judges, need not carry things to their logical conclusion. The people may feel that their disapprobation of homosexual conduct is strong enough to disallow homosexual marriage, but not strong enough to criminalize private homosexual acts—and may legislate accordingly. The Court today pretends that it possesses a similar freedom of action, so that we need not fear judicial imposition of homosexual marriage. At the end of its opinion—after having laid waste the foundations of our rational-basis jurisprudence—the Court says that the present case "does not involve whether the government must give formal recognition to any relationship that homosexual persons seek to enter." Do not believe it. More illuminating than this bald, unreasoned disclaimer is the progression of thought displayed by an earlier passage in the Court's opinion, which notes the constitutional protections afforded to "personal decisions relating to *marriage*, procreation, contraception, family relationships, child rearing, and education," and then declares that "persons in a homosexual relationship may seek autonomy for these purposes, just as heterosexual persons do." Today's opinion dismantles the structure of constitutional law that has permitted a distinction to be made between heterosexual and homosexual unions, insofar as formal recognition in marriage is concerned. If moral disapprobation of homosexual conduct is "no legitimate state interest" for purposes of proscribing that conduct; and if, as the Court coos (casting aside all pretense of neutrality), "when sexuality finds overt expression in intimate conduct with another person, the conduct can be but one element in a personal bond that is more enduring"; what justification could there possibly be for denying the benefits of marriage to homosexual couples exercising "the liberty protected by the Constitution"? Surely not the encouragement of procreation, since the sterile and the elderly are allowed to marry. This case "does not involve" the issue of homosexual marriage only if one entertains the belief that principle and logic have nothing to do with the decisions of this Court. Many will hope that, as the Court comfortingly assures us, this is so.

The matters appropriate for this Court's resolution are only three: Texas's prohibition of sodomy neither infringes a "fundamental right" (which the Court does not dispute), nor is unsupported by a rational relation to what the Constitution considers a legitimate state interest, nor denies the equal protection of the laws. I dissent.

Chapter 6
CRIMINAL AND CIVIL JUSTICE

WEEKS V. UNITED STATES, 232 U.S. 383 (1914)

Fremont Weeks was arrested in Kansas City, Missouri, for operating an illegal lottery. While he was in custody, police officers went to his house, where they were told by a neighbor where Weeks kept a spare key. They used the key to enter his house, searched his room, and took some of his papers. Later they returned, were admitted by a boarder, and found and removed letters from a chest of drawers. The papers and letters were used as evidence against Weeks at his trial. The Supreme Court, in an opinion by Justice William Day, held that the seizure of the papers and letters without a warrant was unconstitutional and, because it was, the evidence could not be used against Weeks at his trial. The Court's opinion created the "exclusionary rule," under which illegally obtained evidence cannot be admitted at trial.

Opinion of the Court by Justice Day:

We shall deal with the Fourth Amendment, which provides:

> The right of the people to be secure in their persons, houses, papers, and effects, against unreasonable searches and seizures, shall not be violated, and no warrants shall issue, but upon probable cause, supported by oath or affirmation and particularly describing the place to be searched, and the persons or things to be seized.

The history of this Amendment is given with particularity in the opinion of Mr. Justice Bradley, speaking for the court in *Boyd v. United States*, 116 U.S. 616 (1886). As was there shown, it took its origin in the determination of the framers of the Amendments to the Federal Constitution to provide for that instrument a Bill of Rights, securing to the American people, among other things, those safeguards which had grown up in England to protect the people from unreasonable searches and seizures, such as were permitted under the general warrants issued under authority of the Government by which there had been invasions of the home and privacy of the citizens and the seizure of their private papers in support of charges, real or imaginary, made against them. Such practices had also received sanction under warrants and seizures under the so-called writs of assistance, issued in the American colonies. Resistance to these practices had established the principle which was enacted into the fundamental law in the Fourth Amendment, that a man's house was his castle and not to be invaded by any general authority to search and seize his goods and papers. "Accordingly," says Lieber in his work on Civil Liberty and Self-Government, 62, in speaking of the English law in this respect, "no man's house can be forcibly opened, or he or his goods be carried away after it has thus been forced, except in cases of felony, and then the sheriff must be furnished with a warrant, and take great care lest he commit a trespass. This principle is jealously insisted upon."

In the *Boyd* case, Mr. Justice Bradley said:

> The principles laid down in this opinion affect the very essence of constitutional liberty and security. They reach farther than the concrete form of the case then before the court, with its adventitious circumstances; they apply to all invasions on the part of the government and its employees of the sanctity of a man's home and the privacies of life. It is not the breaking of his doors, and the rummaging of his drawers, that constitutes the essence of the offence; but it is the invasion of his indefeasible right of personal security, personal liberty and private property, where that right has never been forfeited by his conviction of some public offence,—it is the invasion of this sacred right which underlies and constitutes the essence of Lord Camden's judgment.

In *Bram v. United States*, 168 U.S. 532 (1897), this court said:

> It was in that case demonstrated that both of these Amendments contemplated perpetuating, in their full efficacy, by means of a constitutional provision, principles of humanity and civil liberty, which had been secured in the mother country only after years of

struggle, so as to implant them in our institutions in the fullness of their integrity, free from the possibilities of future legislative change.

The effect of the Fourth Amendment is to put the courts of the United States and Federal officials, in the exercise of their power and authority, under limitations and restraints as to the exercise of such power and authority, and to forever secure the people, their persons, houses, papers and effects against all unreasonable searches and seizures under the guise of law. This protection reaches all alike, whether accused of crime or not, and the duty of giving to it force and effect is obligatory upon all entrusted under our Federal system with the enforcement of the laws. The tendency of those who execute the criminal laws of the country to obtain conviction by means of unlawful seizures and enforced confessions, the latter often obtained after subjecting accused persons to unwarranted practices destructive of rights secured by the Federal Constitution, should find no sanction in the judgments of the courts which are charged at all times with the support of the Constitution and to which people of all conditions have a right to appeal for the maintenance of such fundamental rights.

The case in the aspect in which we are dealing with it involves the right of the court in a criminal prosecution to retain for the purposes of evidence the letters and correspondence of the accused, seized in his house in his absence and without his authority, by a United States Marshal holding no warrant for his arrest and none for the search of his premises. If letters and private documents can thus be seized and held and used in evidence against a citizen accused of an offense, the protection of the Fourth Amendment declaring his right to be secure against such searches and seizures is of no value, and, so far as those thus placed are concerned, might as well be stricken from the Constitution. The efforts of the courts and their officials to bring the guilty to punishment, praiseworthy as they are, are not to be aided by the sacrifice of those great principles established by years of endeavor and suffering which have resulted in their embodiment in the fundamental law of the land. To sanction such proceedings would be to affirm by judicial decision a manifest neglect if not an open defiance of the prohibitions of the Constitution, intended for the protection of the people against such unauthorized action.

MAPP V. OHIO, 367 U.S. 643 (1961)

☞ Following up on a tip, police officers in Cleveland went to Dollree Mapp's house looking for a suspect in connection with a recent crime. Mapp refused them entry because they did not have a warrant, but the officers returned and forced a door open. When Mapp demanded to see a search warrant, an officer held up a piece of paper that he claimed was a warrant. Mapp grabbed it and stuffed it into her shirt, but the officers struggled with her, took back the paper, and handcuffed her. While continuing to search for the suspect, the police rummaged through her closets, dressers, and finally a trunk, in which they found some pornography that she claimed was left by a prior tenant. The suspect was never found, but Mapp was convicted of the possession of obscene material. The Supreme Court, in an opinion by Justice Tom Clark, held that the search was illegal and the exclusionary rule of *Weeks v. Ohio* applied to state as well as federal prosecutions.

Opinion of the Court by Justice Clark:

Seventy-five years ago, in *Boyd v. United States*, 116 U.S. 616 (1886), considering the Fourth and Fifth Amendments as running "almost into each other" on the facts before it, this Court held that the doctrines of those Amendments

> apply to all invasions on the part of the government and its employees of the sanctity of a man's home and the privacies of life. It is not the breaking of his doors, and the rummaging of his drawers, that constitutes the essence of the offence; but it is the invasion of his indefeasible right of personal security, personal liberty and private property. . . . Breaking into a house and opening boxes and drawers are circumstances of aggravation; but any forcible and compulsory extortion of a man's own testimony or of his private papers to be used as evidence to convict him of crime or to forfeit his goods, is within the condemnation (of those Amendments).

The Court noted that "constitutional provisions for the security of person and property should be liberally construed. It is the duty of courts to be watchful for the constitutional rights of the citizen, and against any stealthy encroachments thereon."

In this jealous regard for maintaining the integrity of individual rights, the Court gave life to Madison's prediction that "independent tribunals of justice will be naturally led to resist every encroachment upon rights expressly stipulated for in the Constitution by the declaration of rights."

Since the Fourth Amendment's right of privacy has been declared enforceable against the States through the Due Process Clause of the Fourteenth, it is enforceable against them by the same sanction of exclusion as is used against the Federal Government. Were it otherwise, then, just as without the *Weeks* rule the assurance against unreasonable federal searches and seizures would be "a form of words," valueless and undeserving of mention in a perpetual charter of inestimable human liberties, so too, without that rule, the freedom from state invasions of privacy would be so ephemeral and so neatly severed from its conceptual nexus with the freedom from all brutish means of coercing evidence as not to merit this Court's high regard as a freedom "implicit in the concept of ordered liberty." Therefore, in extending the substantive protections of due process to all constitutionally unreasonable searches—state or federal—it was logically and constitutionally necessary that the exclusion doctrine—an essential part of the right to privacy—be also insisted upon as an essential ingredient of the right. In short, the admission of the constitutional right could not consistently tolerate denial of its most important constitutional privilege, namely, the exclusion of the evidence which an accused had been forced to give by reason of the unlawful seizure. To hold otherwise is to grant the right but, in reality, to withhold its privilege and enjoyment.

Indeed, we are aware of no restraint, similar to that rejected today, conditioning the enforcement of any other basic constitutional right. The right to privacy, no less important than any other right carefully and particularly reserved to the people, would stand in marked contrast to all other rights declared as "basic to a free society." This Court has not hesitated to enforce as strictly against the States as it does against the Federal Government the rights of free speech and of a free press, the rights to notice and to a fair, public trial, including, as it does, the right not to be convicted by use of a coerced confession, however logically relevant it be, and without regard to its reliability. Why should not the same rule apply to what is tantamount to coerced testimony by way of unconstitutional seizure of goods, papers, effects, documents, etc.? We find that, as to the Federal Government, the Fourth and Fifth Amendments and, as to the States, the freedom from unconscionable invasions of privacy and the freedom from convictions based upon coerced confessions do enjoy an "intimate relation" in their perpetuation of "principles of humanity and civil liberty (secured) only after years of struggle."

Moreover, our holding that the exclusionary rule is an essential part of both the Fourth and Fourteenth Amendments is not only the logical dictate of prior cases, but it also makes very good sense.

There are those who say, as did Justice (then Judge) Cardozo, that, under our constitutional exclusionary doctrine, "the criminal is to go free because the constable has blundered." In some cases, this will undoubtedly be the result. But "there is another consideration—the imperative of judicial integrity." The criminal goes free, if he must, but it is the law that sets him free. Nothing can

destroy a government more quickly than its failure to observe its own laws, or worse, its disregard of the charter of
its own existence. As Mr. Justice Brandeis, dissenting, said
in *Olmstead v. United States,* 277 U.S. 438 (1928): "Our
government is the potent, the omnipresent teacher. For
good or for ill, it teaches the whole people by its example.
If the government becomes a lawbreaker, it breeds contempt for law; it invites every man to become a law unto
himself; it invites anarchy."

KYLLO V. UNITED STATES, 533 U.S. 27 (2001)

🖝 Suspicious that Danny Kyllo was growing marijuana
in his home in Oregon, federal agents used a thermal imaging device to see if the heat emissions from the home
were consistent with the high-intensity lamps often
used to grow marijuana indoors. The scan showed that
the garage roof and a side wall were relatively hot, and
the agents used those results to obtain a warrant. When
they searched Kyllo's home, they found marijuana growing. Kyllo was convicted on drug charges. On appeal, the
Supreme Court, in an opinion by Justice Antonin Scalia, held that using the thermal imaging device was a
"search" that was unlawful without a warrant under the
Fourth Amendment.

Opinion of the Court by Justice Scalia:

The Fourth Amendment provides that "[t]he right of
the people to be secure in their persons, houses, papers,

and effects, against unreasonable searches and seizures, shall not be violated." "At the very core" of the Fourth Amendment "stands the right of a man to retreat into his own home and there be free from unreasonable governmental intrusion."

It would be foolish to contend that the degree of privacy secured to citizens by the Fourth Amendment has been entirely unaffected by the advance of technology. The question we confront today is what limits there are upon this power of technology to shrink the realm of guaranteed privacy.

The *Katz* test [is] whether the individual has an expectation of privacy that society is prepared to recognize as reasonable.

[In *Katz v. United States*, 389 U.S. 347 (1967), the Court held: "What a person knowingly exposes to the public, even in his own home or office, is not a subject of Fourth Amendment protection. But what he seeks to preserve as private, even in an area accessible to the public, may be constitutionally protected." Justice John Marshall Harlan, concurring, formulated a famous test for the expectation of privacy:

As the Court's opinion states, "the Fourth Amendment protects people, not places." The question, however, is what protection it affords to those people. Generally, as here, the answer to that question requires reference to a "place." My understanding of the rule that has emerged from prior decisions is that there is a twofold requirement, first that a person have exhibited an actual (subjective) expectation of privacy and, second, that the expectation be one that society is prepared to recognize

as "reasonable." Thus a man's home is, for most purposes, a place where he expects privacy, but objects,
activities, or statements that he exposes to the
"plain view" of outsiders are not "protected" because
no intention to keep them to himself has been exhibited. On the other hand, conversations in the
open would not be protected against being over-
heard, for the expectation of privacy under the circumstances would be unreasonable.]

In the case of the search of a home's interior—the
prototypical and hence most commonly litigated area
of protected privacy—there is a ready criterion, with
roots deep in the common law, of the minimal expectation of privacy that *exists*, and that is acknowledged to
be *reasonable*. To withdraw protection of this minimum
expectation would be to permit police technology to
erode the privacy guaranteed by the Fourth Amendment. We think that obtaining by sense-enhancing
technology any information regarding the home's interior that could not otherwise have been obtained without physical "intrusion into a constitutionally protected
area," constitutes a search—at least where (as here) the
technology in question is not in general public use. This
assures preservation of that degree of privacy against
government that existed when the Fourth Amendment
was adopted. On the basis of this criterion, the information obtained by the thermal imager in this case was
the product of a search.

The Government also contends that the thermal imaging was constitutional because it did not "detect private
activities occurring in private areas." In the home, our

cases show, *all* details are intimate details, because the entire area is held safe from prying government eyes.

GIDEON V. WAINWRIGHT, 372 U.S. 335 (1963)

Clarence Earl Gideon was charged with burglarizing a poolroom in Panama City, Florida. When he was brought to court, without funds and without a lawyer, he asked the court to appoint counsel for him. The trial judge refused because in Florida lawyers were appointed for indigent defendants only in capital cases. During his trial, as the Supreme Court stated, "Gideon conducted his defense about as well as could be expected from a layman," making an opening statement, presenting witnesses, and cross-examining the prosecution's witnesses. Nevertheless, the jury found him guilty, and he was sentenced to five years in the state prison. The Supreme Court, in an opinion by Justice Hugo Black, held that indigent defendants were entitled to have counsel appointed in all serious criminal cases. Gideon was retried and, represented by a lawyer this time, was acquitted.

Opinion of the Court by Justice Black:

The Sixth Amendment provides, "In all criminal prosecutions, the accused shall enjoy the right to have the Assistance of Counsel for his defence."

Reason and reflection require us to recognize that, in our adversary system of criminal justice, any person haled into court, who is too poor to hire a lawyer, cannot be assured a fair trial unless counsel is provided for him. This seems to us to be an obvious truth. Governments, both state and federal, quite properly spend vast sums of money to establish machinery to try defendants accused of crime. Lawyers to prosecute are everywhere deemed essential to protect the public's interest in an orderly society. Similarly, there are few defendants charged with crime, few indeed, who fail to hire the best lawyers they can get to prepare and present their defenses. That government hires lawyers to prosecute and defendants who have the money hire lawyers to defend are the strongest indications of the widespread belief that lawyers in criminal courts are necessities, not luxuries. The right of one charged with crime to counsel may not be deemed fundamental and essential to fair trials in some countries, but it is in ours. From the very beginning, our state and national constitutions and laws have laid great emphasis on procedural and substantive safeguards designed to assure fair trials before impartial tribunals in which every defendant stands equal before the law. This noble ideal cannot be realized if the poor man charged with crime has to face his accusers without a lawyer to assist him. A defendant's need for a lawyer is nowhere better stated than in the moving words of Mr. Justice Sutherland in *Powell v. Alabama*, [287 U.S. 45 (1932)]:

> The right to be heard would be, in many cases, of little avail if it did not comprehend the right to be heard by counsel. Even the intelligent and educated layman has small and sometimes no skill in the science of law. If charged with crime, he is incapable, generally, of deter-

mining for himself whether the indictment is good or bad. He is unfamiliar with the rules of evidence. Left without the aid of counsel, he may be put on trial without a proper charge, and convicted upon incompetent evidence, or evidence irrelevant to the issue or otherwise inadmissible. He lacks both the skill and knowledge adequately to prepare his defense, even though he have a perfect one. He requires the guiding hand of counsel at every step in the proceedings against him. Without it, though he be not guilty, he faces the danger of conviction because he does not know how to establish his innocence.

BODDIE V. CONNECTICUT, 401 U.S. 371 (1971)

☞ Indigent Connecticut residents who sought to file for divorce had their papers rejected by the court clerk because they did not include the required filing fee of $60. They sued in federal court, arguing that preventing them from obtaining a divorce by requiring fees that they could not afford was unconstitutional. The Supreme Court, in an opinion by Justice John Marshall Harlan, held that because family relations were a fundamental right, conditioning divorce on a fee that the residents could not afford violated due process.

Opinion of the Court by Justice Harlan:

At its core, the right to due process reflects a fundamental value in our American constitutional system.

Our understanding of that value is the basis upon which we have resolved this case.

Perhaps no characteristic of an organized and cohesive society is more fundamental than its erection and enforcement of a system of rules defining the various rights and duties of its members, enabling them to govern their affairs and definitively settle their differences in an orderly, predictable manner. Without such a "legal system," social organization and cohesion are virtually impossible; with the ability to seek regularized resolution of conflicts, individuals are capable of interdependent action that enables them to strive for achievements without the anxieties that would beset them in a disorganized society. Put more succinctly, it is this injection of the rule of law that allows society to reap the benefits of rejecting what political theorists call the "state of nature."

American society, of course, bottoms its systematic definition of individual rights and duties, as well as its machinery for dispute settlement, not on custom or the will of strategically placed individuals, but on the common law model. It is to courts, or other *quasi*-judicial official bodies, that we ultimately look for the implementation of a regularized, orderly process of dispute settlement. Within this framework, those who wrote our original Constitution, in the Fifth Amendment, and later those who drafted the Fourteenth Amendment, recognized the centrality of the concept of due process in the operation of this system. Without this guarantee that one may not be deprived of his rights, neither liberty nor property, without due process of law, the state's monopoly over techniques for binding conflict resolution could hardly be said to be acceptable under our scheme of things. Only by providing that the social enforcement mechanism must function strictly within these bounds can we hope to maintain an ordered society that is also just. It is upon this premise that this Court has, through years of adjudication, put flesh upon the due process principle.

As this Court on more than one occasion has recognized, marriage involves interests of basic importance in our society. It is not surprising, then, that the states have seen fit to oversee many aspects of that institution. Without a prior judicial imprimatur, individuals may freely enter into and rescind commercial contracts, for example, but we are unaware of any jurisdiction where private citizens may covenant for or dissolve marriages without state approval. Even where all substantive requirements are concededly met, we know of no instance where two consenting adults may divorce and mutually liberate themselves from the constraints of legal obligations that go with marriage, and, more fundamentally, the prohibition against remarriage, without invoking the state's judicial machinery.

These due process decisions, representing over a hundred years of effort by this Court to give concrete embodiment to this concept, provide, we think, complete vindication for appellants' contentions. In particular, precedent has firmly embedded in our due process jurisprudence two important principles upon whose application we rest our decision in the case before us.

Prior cases establish, first, that due process requires, at a minimum, that, absent a countervailing state interest of overriding significance, persons forced to settle their claims of right and duty through the judicial process must be given a meaningful opportunity to be heard.

What the Constitution does require is "an *opportunity* . . . , granted at a meaningful time and in a meaningful manner, for a hearing appropriate to the nature of the case."

Our cases further establish that a statute or a rule may be held constitutionally invalid as applied when it operates to deprive an individual of a protected right although its general validity as a measure enacted in the legitimate exercise of state power is beyond question.

Drawing upon the principles established by the cases just canvassed, we conclude that the State's refusal to admit these appellants to its courts, the sole means in Connecticut for obtaining a divorce, must be regarded as the equivalent of denying them an opportunity to be heard upon their claimed right to a dissolution of their marriages, and, in the absence of a sufficient countervailing justification for the State's action, a denial of due process.

The arguments for this kind of fee and cost requirement are that the state's interest in the prevention of frivolous litigation is substantial, its use of court fees and process costs to allocate scarce resources is rational, and its balance between the defendant's right to notice and the plaintiff's right to access is reasonable.

In our opinion, none of these considerations is sufficient to override the interest of these plaintiff appellants in having access to the only avenue open for dissolving their allegedly untenable marriages. Not only is there no necessary connection between a litigant's assets and the seriousness of his motives in bringing suit, but it is here beyond present dispute that appellants bring these actions in good faith.

Cover art for the Penguin Civic Classics series draws from early American ephemera and was initially inspired by Benjamin Franklin's "Join, or Die" political cartoon, a woodcut print of a divided snake first published in the *Pennsylvania Gazette* in 1754 to stress the importance of colonial unity. Reinterpreted in modern graphic style, these evocative images and symbols have continued to provoke and inspire into present day.

The text is set primarily in Adobe Caslon, a version of which was used extensively throughout America's colonial period. Indeed, the first printings of the Declaration of Independence and the Constitution were printed in Caslon.